Longman Resources for Instructors

TEACHING ONLINE:
Internet Research, Conversation and Composition

Second Edition

Daniel Anderson, Bret Benjamin,
Christopher Busiel and Bill Paredes-Holt

The University of Texas at Austin

LONGMAN

An imprint of Addison Wesley Longman, Inc.

New York • Reading, Massachusetts • Menlo Park, California • Harlow, England
Don Mills, Ontario • Sydney • Mexico City • Madrid • Amsterdam

Longman Resources For Instructors: Teaching Online: Internet Research, Conversation and Composition, Second Edition

BRIEF CONTENTS

DETAILED CONTENTS

ACKNOWLEDGMENTS FOR THE FIRST EDITION

This book could not have been written without the generous contributions of our colleagues, some of whom helped us specifically in recent weeks, and others from whom we have learned a great deal over the past few years. We'd especially like to thank John Slatin, for providing the supportive environment of the Computer Writing and Research Lab where we work and teach. We'd also like to thank Mike Morrison, for everything and then some. His enduring technical support and editorial advice helped to make this book possible. We are also grateful to the instructors and staff of the Computer Writing and Research Lab, whose friendship and professionalism foster the climate of intellectual discovery and creativity that has made this book possible.

There are a number of people we'd like to thank for providing assistance with various aspects of the publication and design of this book. Thanks to John Ruszkiewicz, who encouraged us to pursue this project and initiated our relationship with HarperCollins (now Longman). Jean Lee Cole provided invaluable advice about design and layout. Xochitl Paredes-Holt meticulously edited our layout and helped design our icons. We should also thank Tonya Browning Westerman who gave up her time to help us choose icon designs. Finally, Amy Strong gave us important advice about the publishing industry and helped us clarify the scope of this project.

We're also indebted to our colleagues who have contributed material to this project. Jean Lee Cole provided input for the case study concerning her class. David Liss took the time to speak with us about his experience using MU* spaces in the classroom. Peg Syverson and Albert Rouzie suggested further readings. Mafalda Stasi, Susan Warshauer and Claire Benedikt provided information about MOO sites and commands.

Most of all, we would like to thank the people closest to us whose support and encouragement have made this work possible. Daniel gives thanks always for Cindy, Peter and Palmer Anderson. Bret thanks Ailise, Woodrow and Clyde Lamoreux for their dogged support. Chris is grateful for the love and patience of Joanne, George and Erika Busiel, and Octavia Kincaid. Bill would like to thank Xochitl Paredes-Holt for her many sacrifices (and for still talking to me).

Chapter One: Introduction

1

The Information Superhighway

entertainment piped into your living room

500 channels *of interactive* edutainment *The Global* VIRTUAL REALITY

The Hive

F i b e r   O p t i c s *Cyberspace* The Information Economy

The Network of Networks VR Logging On

The Electronic Town Hall THE NEW FRONTIER

Multinational Capital and Communications

THE INTERNET

Recent years have seen the Internet receive unparalleled media coverage, touted as an unlimited resource and an egalitarian forum that connects users around the world. Of course if you've tried to get online, you're probably aware that the realities of the Internet don't necessarily match the hype. Resources can be difficult to locate, and the overwhelming amount of vapid, even offensive, information on

1

the Internet can make online experiences disorienting and disturbing. Those who idealistically view the net as egalitarian should also be aware of statistics suggesting that the vast majority of Internet users are white, American males affiliated with institutions of higher education.

Research, Conversation and Composition

While an Internet utopia remains unlikely, there is something about the net that is particularly attractive to teachers of writing. This enormous network does, after all, contain countless texts offering researchers new opportunities for scholarship. For users who are working at home or (perhaps more appropriately for this text) in a computer classroom, the net offers access to documents located around the world. Additionally, the Internet itself can be thought of as an enormous, constantly evolving conversation in which users meet to discuss almost any imaginable topic. This expanded audience gives rise to complex rhetorical situations which can illustrate the practical value of writing skills and provide models for considering effective compositional strategies. There are dozens of ways your class can benefit from using the Internet. Your students could easily:

- access important information. For example, United Nations reports might be used to provide support for an essay about the environmental effects of deforestation on indigenous peoples of the Amazon Basin rain forests.
- talk to authors of class texts or experts in various fields of study.
- meet online with composition classes from different universities to discuss a common text. For example, a project designed to evaluate the multiple perspectives in Spike Lee's film *Do the Right Thing* would be well served by a large pool of knowledgeable participants.
- design and "publish" an interactive, multimedia site on the World Wide Web. For example, students could build a site which examines the effects of economic sanctions on the

dismemberment of South African apartheid, offering a re-search paper, links to further Internet resources about the topic, video clips of major figures, and forums for conversa-tion among users.

Despite the potential advantages of Internet pedagogy and the sig-nificant rise in the number of computer-assisted rhetoric and compo-sition classes, instructors have been surprisingly slow to integrate the tools of the net into their courses. Instructors who teach writing in computer classrooms without using the Internet may be ignoring a particularly valuable tool for improving student composition and criti-cal thinking. Throughout this text we will elaborate on ways the net can bring about this improvement. Initially, we would like to suggest that the Internet facilitates the teaching of four major writing skills.

1. Research Skills: Because of the vast amounts and the wide vari-ety of information that it provides, the Internet can be an excellent means of sharpening research skills. Using the Internet, instructors or students can perform keyword searches on a global scale, or access databases with extensive holdings (see Chapter Five). This wealth of materials necessitates a focused topic, well-evaluated and docu-mented sources, and good strategies for locating information. Addi-tionally, materials found online will in many cases differ a great deal from those found in a library. A student is likely to find resources comprised of new media (graphics, sound and video, for example), or to encounter texts that lack the traditional authority of "published" articles. These new media present students with the challenge and the opportunity to redefine their notion of what constitutes source material.

2. Considering Audience: The Internet offers many instructive opportunities for students to improve their writing by engaging with a larger audience. For example, by participating in a Usenet newsgroup—reading messages carefully, responding, posting questions, and composing longer, well-developed arguments—students can make their ideas public, receive informed feedback, and thereby expand

3

their conception of the requirements of writing for a particular audience (see Chapter Three). Participating in a conversation on the Internet requires students at the very least to compose for a diverse audience, highlighting for them the complexity of rhetorical situations and the importance of good rhetorical strategies.

3. Critical Reading: Because the net contains writing from a wide variety of sources, careful critical reading is necessary. For example, any particular listserv (see Chapter Two) might contain news messages from wire services, in-depth reports from independent journalists or academics who have done a great deal of research on a topic, and any combination of less authoritative messages. Because traditional requirements of expertise do not exist for "publishing," many previously marginalized voices find audiences on the Internet. While increasing the number of perspectives can to some degree democratize access to information, this diversity requires greater attention to source evaluation and provides a more complex understanding of an issue.

4. New Compositional Forms: The Internet can be a particularly useful tool for experimenting with new forms of student composition. The opportunity to construct hypertextual, multimedia projects on the World Wide Web—documents which can organize data, incorporate sound, graphics and video, link to source material located all over the Internet, and provide interactive spaces for audience participation and feedback—allows students to sharpen their rhetorical skills by concentrating on issues of audience, organization and style (see Chapter Six). Similarly, student projects in the text-based "virtual" environments of MU* spaces can help illustrate the importance of descriptive language as well as help teach students how to anticipate audience reaction to their work (see Chapter Four). In either case, asking students to write using new media is an especially effective way to highlight the fluid nature of rhetorical situations and help students envision writing as something more than just rules for five paragraph essays, topic sentences, transitions, and grammar.

Although making distinctions between these four writing skills is pedagogically valuable, the practice of teaching with the Internet works against a simplistic isolation of any of these elements. Conversing in a newsgroup, for example, engages a larger audience, hones critical reading skills, and provides resources. In this text, then, we will discuss the ways that e-mail, Usenet newsgroups, MU* spaces, IRCs, Gopher, and the World Wide Web can be used individually or collectively to strengthen, focus, and complexify a number of student writing skills. We hope that this text will provide the pedagogical insight necessary to incorporate the Internet into existing teaching goals and enough practical knowledge to implement those pedagogical strategies successfully in assignments and exercises.

Some Things To Keep In Mind

As we began to suggest at the opening, there is good cause to critique certain characteristics of the Internet. One of the ways we will consistently try to present critique is through our suggestions that you use the Internet only to the extent that seems merited for your courses. Above all, remember that you don't have to utilize every medium discussed in this book, and that you shouldn't be persuaded to use any of them just because they appear exciting. Similarly, these media can both compound existing instructional problems and introduce new dilemmas. You should be aware of these problems so that you can weigh them against the potential benefits of teaching online, always trying to determine whether the extra work merits the use of Internet media. Some of the problems that we discuss in the following chapters include:

- the initial tendency of students to play online (whether by getting off-task in real-time discussion environments or by surfing the Web for Beavis and Butthead or pornographic materials while they are supposed to be working on research projects).
- the temptation to lose focus on textual composition skills in favor of the excitement of "new forms."

5

- the vast volume of information on the Internet and the possibility for students to get lost.
- the steep learning curve of some applications and Internet technologies.

In tandem with these pedagogical critiques of Internet media, we would also like to present a broader critique of institutional privilege. Within the subset of institutions that have computers available for instruction, a range of different generations of equipment will be in use, and a variety of different setups will be in place for Internet access. We wrote this book primarily for an audience of instructors at institutions like ours, which provide workstation client software for Internet activities (programs on individual computers which provide a user-friendly interface for dealing with the Internet). We realize that not all institutions provide such resources, however, and want to be sensitive to these important differences. At many points throughout the book, we suggest some of the considerations you will have to keep in mind if your institution does not support workstation client software. At the same time, however, we want to recommend strongly that you use client applications. They will make teaching with the Internet a much more manageable task. (See Appendix Five for further information on client software.)

The primary pedagogical concern which grows out of this issue of institutional privilege is that you should try to develop and maintain relationships with the system administrators at your institution. You will receive the best information about available resources from them.

Perhaps more importantly, the question of institutional privilege reflects broader socioeconomic issues about access to the Internet throughout the world. We feel that remaining constantly aware of certain discrepancies, and discussing them with your students, is an important part of using these technologies effectively. Although Internet hosts are spread all over the globe, access to the Internet (and indeed to personal computers in general) is still heavily marked by class, race, gender, and geography.

6

Students should be especially aware of this problem when working on certain research issues, and carefully consider the sources they uncover. For example, there are only a handful of countries with Internet connections in the entire African continent. This discrepancy should complicate our understanding of a newsgroup discussion concerning a particular African nation—who are the people participating in the discussion? What do they have at stake? Which voices are not being heard?

Even if you or your students are not working directly on international topics (or concerns of privilege within the United States), being aware of larger, ongoing issues of access to computer technology is crucial in developing a perspective on work done in the classroom. This critique is one which we would primarily like to point out here in our introduction, since our focus on pedagogical concerns does not allow us to sustain a fully developed materialist critique of Internet access throughout the book.

Strategies for Teaching with the Internet

- Evaluate the time commitments required to implement the technologies effectively.
- Account for different levels of student technological expertise by designing assignments which provide options flexible enough to engage both more experienced students as well as Internet novices. Also, consider forming collaborative groups which can help alleviate discrepancies in student knowledge.
- Try to chart out the territory you plan to introduce to your students before you get to class. Don't assume that the technology will work the way you expect it to. Make sure to check and double check all instructions by walking through the steps before you give your students the assignment.

- Always try to have a backup plan that does not involve using computers in case there are problems with the technology.
- Integrate Internet activities into a well-thought out pedagogy. Don't just use the Internet because it's exciting and different.

What's Ahead

Each of the following chapters contains four major sections: **What, Why, How**, and a **Case Study**. The "What" section provides a brief description of a particular Internet medium, orienting the reader to the key terms and issues which are discussed in the chapter. This section is followed by the "Why" section, which focuses on the broader pedagogical issues of bringing the application into the classroom. The "How" section looks at the challenges of successfully integrating the application into a course and offers tips about how best to create assignments and structure classroom activities. Each "How" section suggests techniques and exercises you can use to introduce your students to each of the Internet media, and concludes with several more complex writing assignments utilizing the Internet. Finally, the "Case Study" offers an in-depth look at an actual assignment in which students use the medium to further their rhetorical and compositional skills.

Chapter Two discusses working with e-mail. We consider e-mail to be the building block of Internet communication, a tool that can transform the daily operations of the classroom. Our third chapter looks at Usenet newsgroups, focusing on the benefits of an expanded audience for student writing and emphasizing the importance of critical reading skills. Chapter Four discusses IRC lines and MU* spaces, text-based media which allow "real-time" conversation and the construction of virtual environments. Chapter Five looks at "browsing" the Internet for resources. We will consider a variety of strategies for successfully finding and evaluating Internet research materials. Our final chapter looks at ways instructors can use the World Wide Web to get their classes online. This chapter examines how your courses can integrate the challenges of hypertextual composition by having your students publish multimedia documents on the Web.

Chapter One: Introduction

Chapter Two
Initiating Conversation:
E-Mail

2

WHAT IS E-MAIL?

If the Internet can be described as a continuously evolving conversation, then e-mail is the basic technology that allows you to speak up and be heard. We see e-mail as the building block of Internet communication and composition.

In this chapter, we will consider how electronic correspondence can transform the daily operations of the classroom. We will look at ways that e-mail focuses attention on audience and facilitates contact between students and instructors. We will also discuss using e-mail to expand the traditional boundaries of the classroom, by bringing outside voices into discussions, and by increasing research possibilities. These movements not only greatly improve students' ability to gather resources and engage in discussion, but also provide some interesting ways to explore issues of audience, tone, and style.

We also want to suggest that the conversational nature of e-mail makes it especially valuable to teachers of writing. Discussion facilitated through e-mail moves between message and response with the spontaneity of conversation; however, a student can take as much time as needed to compose a message or response. Further, message archival makes it easy to recall and critique a forgotten point or important comment and turns messages into potential course resources.

The rest of this chapter will discuss the importance of e-mail to our teaching, and offer strategies for using it in the classroom. We conclude with a case study detailing the electronic correspondence between students and the author of a course text.

Key Terms

Domain: an element of an Internet or e-mail address designating an Internet organization, sub-organizations and the type of organization (e.g., *widgetinc.com*, or *utexas.edu*).

Flame: usually a pejorative term describing a post that attacks a message or an individual. A flame usually has a confrontational tone and offers little or no constructive criticism.

Listserv: also known as a "mailing list" or "list." A program which allows mail to be sent to a group of addresses at once.

Mail Reader: also known as a "mail client." A program which provides an easy interface for reading, composing, posting and downloading e-mail messages.

Mail Server: an Internet server which organizes, stores and distributes e-mail messages.

Mailbox: the specific identification or name given to an e-mail user. Used in conjunction with the domain name, it makes up the e-mail address.

Nickname: similar to an address book entry for storing one or more e-mail addresses. When a message is sent to the nickname, the computer sends that message to each of the addresses in the nickname file.

WHY USE E-MAIL?

Addressing Your Audience

E-mail offers instructors and students an excellent opportunity to think through the rhetorical significance of audience. E-mail requires an author to define a readership, both in the way the message can be addressed to one or multiple people, and in the way the message addresses the concerns particular to that audience. The audience for e-mail messages can encompass a single instructor or student, a group of students, the class as a whole, a campus e-mail discussion list, or a worldwide audience made up of personal contacts or subscribers to a listserv. Whatever the scope of the interaction, students will at least have considered their audience before hitting the "send" button.

By putting students on listservs—mailing lists which send messages to multiple recipients—instructors can tap into discussion groups which exist outside the classroom. (Throughout this text, we will use the term *listserv* generically to denote a range of mailing list programs including Listserv, Majordomo and Listproc.) Students using these lists must learn to interact with a large audience and to take into account the previous discussions on the list.

Though listservs vary according to function, type and administration, each listserv has a very narrowly defined subject area that subscribers are expected to adhere to in their posts. Additionally, students must consider conventions of Internet etiquette, or "netiquette." One does not usually send a message to a list just to pass the time or to try to sell a car (unless, of course, the list is for the purpose of selling used cars). For most lists, posts like this would be frowned upon and result in a number of angry messages from list members (commonly referred to as flames). Some lists have moderators who screen messages before sending them to the full list, in order to ensure their relevance. Repeated inflammatory or "off-topic" messages from a user can result in removal from the list.

A class might use a list to analyze how messages stay "on-topic" and how well they appeal to the list's audience. By following a listserv discussion, students can determine the nature of the listserv's audience, eventually learning what constitutes an interesting or convincing message. Sometimes, the boundaries of allowable topics on a list are very narrowly defined. For example, the **h-latam** list (a discussion of Latin American history) specifically defines its subject to exclude current events in Latin America. Because the list perceives its function as providing a levelheaded discussion of "historical" events, especially as these relate to teaching history, potentially heated political discussions of more recent events in Latin America are therefore discouraged. A post discussing causes and effects of the Zapatista uprising in Chiapas, Mexico, for instance, would not be allowed on the list unless it was directed solely to bibliographic source material or pedagogical concerns. Analyzing these divisions in the purpose and content of writing can provide very useful demonstrations for your students.

Forms and Formality

The "basic" nature of e-mail lends itself to a study of the many levels of formality in composition. Because of its very powerful ability to cover spatial distances quickly, e-mail is often the best way to drop a quick note to someone online, to make sure that a message is seen by an instructor or a student, or to have students submit a graded composition. This multifaceted communication medium requires students to move skillfully between different levels of formality.

By its nature, e-mail tends to be less formal than traditional composition. Messages often contain unedited typographical errors, informal acronyms like BTW (by the way), FWIW (for what it's worth) or IMHO (in my humble opinion), and abbreviations like msg (message), mtg (meeting) or shd (should). The ability to send and receive messages quickly by using e-mail has de-emphasized the importance of the carefully constructed prose generally found in other forms of correspondence. In fact, e-mail can be compared more closely with spoken conversation than with its more obvious counterpart, letter writing. However, since e-mail lacks certain qualities of face-to-face interaction—gestures, mannerisms, intonations—electronic conversationalists have developed additional conventions for expressing these non-textual cues. Phenomena like emoticons, signature files, and reply quotations become increasingly important in a textual online world.

Expressing sarcasm and lighthearted emotion is often achieved by using emoticons (usually called "smileys"). Though they often denote the lack of careful writing that irony requires, smileys do communicate something about the author's intention. The basic smiley is a sideways happy face :-) although a whole host of others can be used to express a broad range of emotions. While we wouldn't recommend teaching these symbols as part of formal writing, instructors and students should understand that manipulating these forms is part of e-mail communication. Distinguishing between the ability to incorporate a smiley in informal prose and the necessity of carefully constructing irony in a formal composition can also be an important lesson.

A Small Sampling of Smileys.

:-)	basic smiley	C=:-)	chef smiley
;-)	winking happy smiley	X:-)	little kid with a propeller beanie
;-(	crying smiley		
:-{	mustache	[:-)	smiley wearing a walkman
:-}X	bow tie-wearing smiley	8(:-)	Mickey Mouse
@:-}	smiley just back from the hairdresser	:——}	you lie like pinnochio

Taken from "scarecrows ascii funnies,"

ftp://ftp.wwa.com/pub/Scarecrow/Misc/Smilies

Another widely utilized way of personalizing e-mail communication is by adding a "signature" or "sig file" to a message. A signature is a section of text automatically appended to the bottom of e-mail messages. Signatures serve as a way to identify the author and place him socially, professionally, and personally. Besides supplying the writer's e-mail address to facilitate replies, a signature will often carry a writer's professional or academic affiliations, an indication of whether the current message is personal or professional, or a favorite quotation. To enhance the rather dry nature of this information, many authors have developed elaborate arrangements of ASCII text and symbols in their signatures.

Although the convention is widespread, the use of signature files has not been wholly accepted by all Internet users. As a result, plays upon the signature file abound. One of the most succinct signature files, dutifully attached at the end of many messages, is "This is not a signature."

```
(" `_' '_/" ).___. __.' .. ._JohnDoe@mail.utexas.edu
    `6_ 6  )  `-. (      ). `-.__. ` )      John Doe
    (_Y_.)'  ._   )  ` _ `. `` _.__._.' Department of
_..`--'_.. _-_/ /--'_.' ,               Nomenclature
(i I ),-'' (I i),' ((!.-'
```

ASCII Art in a signature file

Another e-mail convention is the reply quotation, which also occurs only because of the ease with which computer technology reproduces text. When you reply to an e-mail message, you usually get the opportunity to include the original message in the response. However, because of the difficulty of carefully situating quotes inside your own text, the e-mail convention for quoting text uses a greater-than symbol (>) to indicate the text that is quoted from the original message. Because most mail readers will automatically put the whole text of the message into a response, reply quotations are often quite long and include lots of extraneous information.

Messages which have been forwarded or quoted a number of times will place additional (>) symbols before each line of the quoted text. This nesting of quotations continues until one of the readers decides that there is no need to include the older text. Because e-mail messages are read with varying frequency by different users, some feel it necessary to include the original question or issue for clarity. While an unnecessarily long reply quotation can be an annoyance, it can be useful to "overhear" part of the original conversation, or to analyze the original message a second time.

E-mail provides a unique opportunity to discuss levels of formality in writing. Messages always have a purpose that in some sense determines their tone and form. Students can respond to potentially offensive posts with a very formal and distanced stance if they wish

```
            To: student@mail.utexas.edu
          From: instructor@mail.utexas.edu
       Subject: Re:  Can we meet?
            Cc:
           Bcc:
   Attachments:
..........................................................................
   >Howdy Instructor,
   >
   >I was writing to see if we could set up
   >a meeting to talk about the paper that's
   >due on Friday. I have to work on Tuesday
   >during your office hours, so I was wondering
   >if we could set up a time on Wednesday?  You
   >can mail me back or call at 555-5000. Thanks.
   >
   >John Doe

   No problem John.  I can meet with you in the
   morning between 9 and 10:30 or in the
   afternoon after 2:00.  Drop me a line and tell
   me if either of those times is OK with you.

   Instructor
```

Quoted text in an e-mail reply

to diffuse anger but not ignore a contested issue. They can also heighten the conflict by responding very personally and antagonistically. Although students generally learn the necessity of using tone carefully in their e-mail communication, they may have difficulty incorporating that knowledge into their formal writing assignments. By moving between formal and informal writing in e-mail, you can help your students translate the skills they develop in informal writing to their formal work.

Learning to Talk, Talking to Learn

Joining conversations outside of the classroom shows students that writers can be committed to the discussion of issues and ideas and demonstrates that student writing can have an importance in a larger context. Using listservs can give students access to the opinions of experts. This access to information is a useful stimulus for generating a topic and finding a way to enter a conversation. For example, depending on the listserv, students might come across an index of sources about a research topic or gather extremely current information on a contemporary debate or event.

As we demonstrate below in "Gathering Resources," there are a variety of resources that can be accessed through electronic mail, many of which differ from traditional research materials. The multiplicity of voices in listserv debates provides valuable teaching tools and uncommon student resources. Instructors can emphasize the need for critical reading in evaluating these sources, while students can see both the importance of the issues to those individuals engaged in the list discussion and the importance of the rhetorical skills they are being taught in class.

Besides drawing upon the conversations of subscribers to a list, e-mail offers the ability to interact with members of the list. Students can ask questions, post their own opinions and receive reactions to the arguments they make. This interaction exposes students to perspectives outside of the classroom and highlights the need for students to write clearly, responsibly and knowledgeably. If a student's message asks an obvious question or appears to ask the list subscribers to do the student's research for them, the message will likely receive some hostile responses and few, if any, useful replies. But if students are able to engage the audience with either an interesting argument or an important category of research or analysis, they will likely receive many useful citations and suggestions for further thought. Because of the nature of electronic communication, all of these messages can easily be archived on a diskette and retrieved for later use. Messages can also be forwarded to an instructor, other students, or people outside the classroom.

HOW CAN YOUR CLASS USE E-MAIL?————

Getting Connected

Since e-mail is extremely important to class communication, we recommend that all students set up an account. Most colleges and universities have already incorporated computer and Internet fees into tuition costs, so they generally offer "free" or very inexpensive e-mail accounts to students and faculty.

Although setting up an account is usually a fairly simple process, some students will inevitably have problems along the way. Remember that for many students, this will be the first time they have ever tried to use computers for anything besides word processing and that there is a certain amount of technophobia to be overcome.

Addresses and Their Elements

A typical e-mail address contains two elements. The mailbox name or user's name appears before the @ sign, and the domain information follows the @ sign. A sample message might use the addresses:

From: bozo@archives.widgetinc.com
To: bilbo@mail.utexas.edu

The mailbox name of the sender is bozo. The recipient's mailbox name is bilbo; both are served mail from their respective domains.

The domain generally contains information about the organization and organization type. Elements of the domain are separated by a period (.) generally called a "dot".

In the sample, we have the machine name, "archives," the name of the organization, "widgetinc" and an abbreviation describing the type of organization, "com" (commercial). The recipient of the message has the mailbox name "bilbo," operated by the machine named "mail," registered with the organization "utexas," classified as "edu" (educational).

In the United States, the standard domain types are

.edu = educational institution
.com = commercial organization
.gov = government organization
.mil = military institution

Outside the United States, domain names usually end in a two-letter element indicating the country of origin: for example, .jp (Japan), .nl (the Netherlands), and .eg (Egypt).

Setting up accounts often takes a little longer than you might expect. We suggest that you have your students request accounts very early in the semester—before the second class period if possible—so that the university will have time to process the requests, and students will be able to activate their accounts within the first week or two of the semester. We also suggest that you patiently walk your students through the process to make sure that everyone is connected. The best way to do this is to write up a handout with detailed step-by-step instructions. Since universities frequently change mail account procedures from semester to semester as they expand their computer services, you should double check that all of your instructions are correct. If you are teaching in a computer classroom, you might plan to use half or even a full class period making sure that all of your students' accounts are set up. If you are teaching in a traditional classroom, we recommend that you set up a tutorial session for those students who feel uncomfortable with the process.

21

Mail Readers and Servers

Mail servers are programs which reside on Internet-connected machines which store and distribute electronic messages. A user has three basic options for accessing these servers:

- The most basic, but also the most limited, way to work with e-mail is through a connection to a remote machine's mail server via a Telnet client. It is possible to read and send messages with this connection; the interface, however, is quite awkward.

- Most users will prefer to use a mail reading client when working with e-mail. Making a Telnet connection to a remote machine and activating a mail reading client provides an easier interface and offers more features to the user than connecting directly to the mail server.

- Workstation mail reading clients reside on the user's personal computer and provide the most versatile interface for handling e-mail operations. These programs (Eudora is probably the most popular and is available as freeware) retrieve mail from the mail server and bring it to a user's machine. New messages are easily composed, edited, sent and saved. Mail readers generally allow users to create nicknames and offer features like the ability to send formatted documents and organize incoming mail into directories or folders for later use.

(See Appendix Five for more client/server information.)

If your students are using a server-based client application (like Pine, for Unix servers), their messages will remain on the server until deleted, and they will also be able to create folders within their mail account, to sort messages they wish to save for future reference. You will have to familiarize students with the keystroke commands of these server-based clients; in Pine, for example, users type "c" to begin composing a new message, "i" for "folder index" (to view the contents of the current folder), and "l" for "folder list" (to select a different folder).

If your students are instead using a workstation-based client like Eudora, they will additionally have to configure a settings file, which they will probably keep on a diskette along with the mail that they download from their account. These settings are easily configured, and once the student's information (like the return address, signature file, and the domain name of the mail server) is entered, it will never again have to be retyped. You will also want to familiarize your students with other features of workstation mail clients. Looking at a portion of a sample composition window, note a number of these features:

By clicking on items across the top bar, the user can set such features as "text-wrap" at the end of lines, as well as automatically save a copy of the message in her outgoing mailbox, and control whether or not to use her signature file (which Eudora saves in another window). The button which reads "queue" files this outgoing message for mailing, but it will not be sent until the user selects a menu command to send all her queued messages. This feature is useful to minimize the time one is actually connected to the Internet (if a modem and a phone share the same line, for example, or your Internet access is billed by the minute). If the user were to change a particular setting, the "queue" button would instead say "send," and clicking it would deliver the message immediately.

To verify that the accounts are working, have students send themselves a test message. Students who receive their own test message can be sure that the account is working. After this initial test is done, have students send a message to you so that you can compile a list of class e-mail addresses, and keep track of who is connected.

E-Mail in the Classroom: Step-by-Step

1. Familiarize yourself with the process of establishing e-mail accounts at your institution, and walk your students through this process during the first week of class.
2. Introduce your students to the mail reader they will be using. If they will utilize a workstation-based client application, have them create a settings file on a diskette, to which they will also download their e-mail throughout the semester.
3. Assign your students the task of sending themselves a test message to make sure their accounts are working properly.
4. Assign your students the task of sending you a preliminary message. From these messages, compile a directory of student e-mail addresses.
5. E-mail to your students the list of addresses for the class, and walk them through the process of making from this list a class nickname in their mail reader.
6. Establish a listserv for your course (optional, depending on institutional resources and course needs).

Once all of your students have activated their accounts, the next step will probably be to create a class listserv or a class nickname file so that you and your students will be able to share messages with the class as a whole. If you have easy access to a host computer that has been set up to run listserv software, then the most efficient way of communicating with your class will be to have your students subscribe to a class listserv. However, since most instructors won't have easy access to a listserv machine, using your mail reader to create a class nickname file—a list of your class's e-mail addresses separated by commas—will work just as effectively. This way when you or one of your students wants to send a message to the entire class, the message can be sent to the listserv or the nickname file rather than each address individually having to be typed.

We have found that class listservs or nicknames are extremely useful. Instructors can make announcements, revise reading or meeting schedules, forward supplementary material, start discussion, or ask for feedback on a particular topic. Lists and nicknames also give students the opportunity to contribute material for course reading and to share relevant resources with the entire class.

E-mail can also facilitate course operation by linking up members of the class on an individual basis and giving students "immediate" access to the instructor outside of class and office hours. Students faced with an unexpected problem or question can e-mail their instructor as soon as that problem arises, and know that the instructor will respond reasonably quickly. Additionally, students who may be reluctant to come to office hours often feel more comfortable sending an e-mail message. Although e-mail communication does not take the place of personal interaction with your students, it offers instructors the advantage of being able to respond promptly but thoroughly to student questions, perhaps even by including an article or citation in the reply.

This enhanced contact between instructors and individual students can be utilized in any number of ways throughout a semester. Students who miss class or who have a question about an assignment can easily e-mail questions to their instructor. Students can use e-mail to turn in papers or other homework assignments, to which instructors can respond by e-mailing comments back to the student. Instructors can forward materials particularly relevant to one student's project or get in touch with students to ask questions or work out problems. For all of these reasons, e-mail has become central to the daily operations of our classes.

Think pedagogically about the ways that e-mail can be utilized by your students. We have found that e-mail is an invaluable tool for helping coordinate any number of group activities:

- Peer review partners can e-mail each other their drafts and comments with the advantage of being able to ask questions and carry on a dialogue.
- Small groups working on collective projects can use e-mail to brainstorm about ideas, to share work that they have completed individually, or to coordinate times to meet as a group.
- Students who have similar research topics can use e-mail to exchange resources and materials that they may have found.

Depending upon the nature of the assignments and the structure of your class, e-mail can effectively enhance different types of collective work among your students.

Gathering Resources

In addition to enhancing communication between instructors and students, e-mail can serve as a research tool for students. Although it may not be as powerful as some of the utilities we will discuss in later chapters, e-mail can be effectively worked into a research curriculum.

The first, and probably the most important, of the ways that e-mail can be applied to research is by subscribing to listservs. We've already discussed how listservs facilitate communication within the classroom, but listservs which have much wider subscription circles can be an important way both to gather resource materials and to get a sense of the range of positions on a given issue. Students can subscribe to any of literally thousands of topic-based listservs according to their own personal interests, or coinciding with course topics. These lists range in traffic anywhere from one message every six months to fifty or more per day. The types of information posted on lists also vary widely; some lists limit themselves to news stories and articles, while others are dedicated solely to discussion.

As a result, it is difficult to judge what traits certain lists might have before subscribing. This uncertainty presents some obvious problems for instructors as they try to determine what lists might be the most productive for their students, especially if they are hoping to steer different students to different lists depending upon individual research topics. There is no completely satisfactory solution to this dilemma. We have found that colleagues who work in a field which coincides with a student project will often have helpful suggestions about good listservs in that area or discipline. Also, the Web site *http://tile.net/listserv/* contains some useful information about a number of listservs (see Chapter Five for information about finding resources on the World Wide Web).

Although these descriptions are a helpful start, you may want to subscribe to the list yourself, or simply trust the judgment of your students and allow them to decide for themselves the quality and usefulness of any particular list.

As a cautionary note, we recommend that you prepare your students before they join a listserv. Many listservs frown upon full classes participating in the list, so you should, if possible, post a message asking listserv members about having your students join. Additionally, students should spend time reading the list, or "lurking," before

PHIL-LIT

Philosophy and Literature

Country: **USA**

Site: **Texas A&M University**

Computerized administrator: **listserv@listserv.tamu.edu**

Human administrator: **phil-lit-request@listserv.tamu.edu**

You can join this group by sending the message "*sub PHIL-LIT your name*" to **listserv@listserv.tamu.edu**

Online description of a listserv taken from http://tile.net/listserv/

they attempt to join the conversation. Since many students get discouraged when faced with an overly hostile response to their first postings, instructors should stress the importance of preparing messages carefully.

Listservs can be applied pedagogically in a variety of ways. In terms of gathering substantive research material, those lists which primarily post items like news stories, articles, documents, and expert commentary will probably be the most useful. However, you should not give up on a list simply because it focuses on discussion. Meaningful insight into a topic can be gained by following the various threads of discussion on a list. We ask our students to keep track of and participate in active listserv debates so that they may witness the ways in which opinions are formed, revised, and complicated on the list. When students have examined this dialogue critically, we find that their writing often reflects the multiple perspectives on a topic that a listserv discussion can illustrate, revealing the ways that collaborative debate can form and inform student composition. Also discuss various issues of netiquette with students before having them subscribe to a list.

As a corollary to the idea of list messages being shaped to particular audiences, we find that discussion lists provide an excellent opportunity for instructors to demonstrate the importance of critical reading. Because of the nontraditional nature of some e-mail "sources," students are forced to examine and analyze both the content and the style of listserv postings. We recommend that you cull a selection of messages from a listserv discussion to help illustrate the skills of critical reading and source evaluation, perhaps by focusing the discussion on the importance of writing for a particular audience. We find that because students see in these public debates practical applications of the rhetorical skills we teach in class, convincing them that these skills are important becomes a much easier task.

Along with the research possibilities provided by listservs, e-mail can be an effective tool for transferring and gathering other types of information. For instance, many online library catalogues and databases have implemented features that allow users to mail information to their accounts. Students who find useful online articles or encyclopedia entries can collect that information easily by e-mailing themselves the material. Once the student receives the material in electronic form, she can refer back to the piece at a later date, or cut and paste quotations into a research paper.

Expanding the Classroom

As we suggested above, e-mail offers opportunities to move beyond the limitations of the classroom. By using e-mail to connect your class with a larger audience, you will provide your students with a way to learn from the expertise and creative thinking of a wider pool of knowledge.

Connecting different sections of the same course is one productive method of expanding the classroom. There are a number of ways that successful collaboration can occur between classes working on similar issues or similar texts. Students can be effectively grouped across sections according to similar topic interests. Conversely, we have also found that sparking debates by grouping students working on opposing positions can help refine their arguments in order to take other points of view into account. Keep in mind the fact that altering the number of students involved in the groups will produce very different kinds of collaboration.

Along the same lines, linking interested students at multiple institutions can offer further pedagogical advantages. Instructors often send requests on listservs or newsgroups (see Chapter Three) about linking up classes in different parts of the country or world. Whether these requests are specifically designed to connect classes working on similar material, or whether the instructors are just hoping to have their students work on developing a personal voice through less formal correspondence, these kinds of e-mail connections can add significantly to a course. One way of making contacts with instructors seeking partner classes for e-mail exchanges is the International E-Mail Classroom Connections mailing list. To subscribe, and find out more information, send a message containing the word "subscribe" to *iecc-request@stolaf.edu*.

Finally, e-mail can be effectively used by connecting students to guest participants. Instructors who are in correspondence with particular authors or critics may be able to conduct a series of exchanges between the class and experts who would broaden the students' perspectives on the texts being studied. This strategy is the focus of this chapter's Case Study.

Because of its ease and flexibility, e-mail offers instructors and students a communications medium which can be tailored according to the instructor's pedagogical goals. It provides a simple and effective means of communicating that can be extremely useful in the daily operations of running a class. E-mail also has important applications for the instructor who is interested in either online research or expanding the boundaries of the classroom. We have found that in many ways e-mail is central to the daily operation of our classes, and we highly recommend that instructors (whether or not they are teaching in a computer-assisted classroom) experiment with ways of working this powerful tool into their teaching practice.

Introductory Exercises: E-Mail

• As soon as their e-mail accounts are set up, have students send a test message to themselves, both to practice the mail composition process and to ensure the accounts are working properly. • Compile and distribute a directory of student e-mail addresses; introduce students to the "nickname" feature in their mail reader by instructing them how to make a nickname from the directory list. • Incorporate e-mail exchange into your pre-existing collaborative assignments, such as peer review. • Assign students regular postings to the class listserv: responses to discussion or readings, written assignments, research findings, etc. (consider a portfolio system to grade listserv postings).

Sample Assignments

• Have students in peer review groups e-mail papers and peer reviews to each other. Instead of writing a single peer review, have your students go through at least one more round of follow-up responses. This will give the author of a paper a chance to ask peer reviewers questions about their suggestions or about effective ways of incorporating the changes suggested in the review. Have students send a copy of their reviews to the instructor as well.

• Have students subscribe to a listserv. After they have followed the conversation for about a week, have them write

31

up a short description of the listserv, analyzing the audience, the listserv's main function, the types of messages posted to the listserv, or any other distinguishing characteristics.

- Collect several messages from a listserv discussion which demonstrate an array of positions on a given subject. Forward these messages to your students as class reading and suggest that they look for the various rhetorical strategies in each posting. Have a class discussion about the listserv's probable audience and how authors shape their messages to accommodate a particular readership. Use this as an opportunity to teach critical reading skills and to demonstrate to your students the ways that nontraditional sources can be used effectively to support an argument.

- Using a contact that you already have, or after establishing a contact through a listserv, a newsgroup (see Chapter Three) or a Web page (see Chapter Five), connect your class to a class in another part of the country or world. You can use this connection to talk about texts or issues that may be of shared interest to both classes. Or perhaps, if the students are from different cultures, correspondence may provide students with insights into the cultural assumptions that shape arguments.

E-MAIL CASE STUDY
E309K The Rhetoric of New Realities
Instructor: Christopher Busiel

This case study demonstrates how you might involve an outside participant in some aspect of your courses. In this particular case, the participant was the author of a course text. An exercise like the one described below creates a new kind of rhetorical situation for your students, gives them a particular audience to envision, and focuses the need for a certain kind of expertise with the course material. One of the end results of such an exercise is that students gain a deeper knowledge about a particular text or topic, using their rhetorical skills to uncover a layer of understanding they might not otherwise have reached.

At the University of Texas, instructors use "Topics in Writing" courses to explore the connection between critical reading and writing. "The Rhetoric of New Realities" examined the way in which the philosophical idea of "reality" (comprising such issues as cognition, perspective, representation) is constructed by language and is, we might say, a function of rhetoric. One of the important texts in this course was Terence McKenna's collection of essays *The Archaic Revival*.

McKenna began his career in the field of ethnobotany, studying the use of psychedelic plants in cultures whose religions are based around shamanic ritual. The cultural means by which reality is defined are quite important to him. Additionally, he explores such philosophical problems as the role of language in the creation of reality, the nature of pre-linguistic cognition, the possibility of a technological means of communication beyond language, and the ontological status of the UFO. McKenna's texts enabled the instructor to get his students to explore the question of how an author uses the tools of rhetoric to try to prove points for which his audience must have very little frame of reference, indeed which may challenge their very foundations of belief.

33

The students were assigned to work in small groups (either in pairs or threes) and to post a message to McKenna, asking the author several questions about his text. In this case, group work served not only to allow the students to develop ideas in conversation with one another, but to relieve some of the work from the guest participant, giving him only seven or eight messages to answer instead of twenty-one. The students were asked to take advantage of the opportunity of speaking with an author to raise issues which were not directly answerable in the text, to request further discussion of a particular issue, or to raise oppositional points if they had them. The only other instruction they were given was to remember to project a strong ethos, by being polite to their guest (especially if they were critiquing him) and by making very clear the context for each of their questions, showing McKenna they had thought about his writing carefully, and grounding their comments in references to specific passages.

The students were all very comfortable with e-mail by this point in the semester, so the instructor simply sent McKenna's address and the rather brief assignment summary to the class list. He also asked the students to send him a copy of their messages to McKenna, in order to review what they had written. The instructor also stayed in close e-mail contact with McKenna the week before the exchange of messages, to work out all of the details and ensure that nothing would go wrong.

Overall, students responded well to the rhetorical situation created by the exercise. They had insightful observations about the material, and demonstrated an understanding of certain rhetorical concepts from the course, especially ethos. Several students used the opportunity to question McKenna's own rhetorical strategies, aware that his use of difficult vocabulary and dense compositional style constructs a very particular, perhaps educationally elitist, audience. "If McKenna can make the point much more directly," they had queried in class, "why doesn't he?" The fact that they had the opportunity to pose such questions to the author himself demonstrates perhaps better than any other element of this case study the undeniable value of using e-mail to place students into new rhetorical situations.

The selections below, from the dialogue which developed between McKenna and the students, demonstrate thoughtful analysis on the part of the students. (Note: the excerpts from the e-mail exchanges are reproduced verbatim; mechanical errors have not been edited.)

This student's message presents a courteous ethos in its consideration for the time and energy McKenna has given to the course. The first question she poses explores a connection between McKenna's writing and another text:

> My class here at the University of Texas has
> had the pleasure of studying your book, _The
> Archaic Revival_, and I am delighted to have
> the opportunity to communicate with you via
> Internet. In familiarizing myself with your
> work, I must say I have needed to stop every
> few pages to take a deep breath or two, as
> your speculations are not only overwhelming
> and well-founded, but in my opinion, ex-
> tremely revolutionary - perhaps a bible of
> sorts for the 21st century. I would like to
> pose a few questions to you concerning this
> book. Please respond at your convenience.
> In reading, I kept thinking of _Celestine
> Prophecy_, by James Redfield. Are you fa-
> miliar with this text? Specifically, on
> page 59 of _The Archaic Revival_ in your
> discussion of UFOs, you mention the idea of
> a collective psyche. Redfield touches on
> this as well, in a fictitious manner, yet he
> claims that most of the book is filled with
> actual theories and experiences he has had.

She concludes this point by asking for more detail about McKenna's comments about a collective unconscious, and his seeming implication that it is the domain of cultures based in certain kinds of ritual. "How," she asks, "do you feel about the idea of a collective mind in the context of America?" McKenna responds:

```
My notion of the collective psyche is
closely related to the concept of the col-
lective unconscious developed by C. G. Jung.
It is the notion of a kind of genetic mind
or memory that is deeper than cultural con-
ditioning and hence is shared by all human
beings in all times and places.  I have not
read Redfied's book, the aura around it
being too commercial and new agey for me.
As for the American collective psyche. . .
the human mass psyche generally is becoming
explicit through the technological innova-
tion of the Internet and the World Wide Web.
These are material manifestations of the
presence of the collective overmind of the
species.
```

Another student, feeling that McKenna condemns science too broadly in his claims that a scientific view of the world has brought us to the brink of ecological disaster, asks for further clarification and counters with an interpretation driven by personal investment, but also based in careful rhetorical analysis:

```
You say on page 61(ch 5):

'The UFO is an idea intended to confound
science, because science has begun to
threaten the existence of the human species
as well as the ecosystem of the planet.'
This is a very strongly negative view of
science, I think, and that is okay to feel
that way.  However, a problem arises in my
```

eyes when you go on later in the book (in ch
15, 'Plan/Plant/Planet') to describe many
interesting methods of how man might revi-
talize planet earth. Being quite the tree-
hugger myself, I like very much the ideas
that you present, but none of these things
can be accomplished without knowledge and
skills acquired through science. For example, nanotechnology, large-scale recy-
cling, and photovoltaic cells [*all of which
McKenna discusses in this chapter*] are answers that will never be practically fea-
sible without the same kind of study and
learning that found them in the first place:
scientific and technological research. I
think that perhaps you have misplaced the
blame of the possible downfall of mankind on
scientists alone.... After all, Einstein
did NOT discover relativity so America could
blow Hiroshima off of the map. It was government that did that destruction.

In response to this comment McKenna explains:

This is an important point. Notice your
examples: nanotechnology, large-scale recy-
cling, and photovoltaic cells. These are
the products of applied science, in other
words, technology. My criticism is not of
technology, it is a deeper criticism of
science, it is a criticism of scientific
method and its operational belief, called
Reductionism, that nature is to be understood through analysis of successively
smaller and smaller parts. The overlooking
of the function of whole systems and of the
seamless quality of nature, especially biology, has given us a mechanistic and spirit-
less biology that is now at the end of its

career as an explanatory engine. For more
on this check out Rupert Sheldrake's _The
Rebirth of Nature_.

A third student questions the radical nature of McKenna's rhetoric
(and its possible effects) more broadly:

> I am sure you are aware that these ideas are
> at the very least original and many conser-
> vative Christians might say unbelievable,
> but do you feel that by addressing your
> beliefs with out regard to exactly how the
> public will respond you make your positions
> that much more palatable to twentieth cen-
> tury society? Almost as though by making
> available an extreme you draw more people to
> the middle of the road? [. . . .] By pre-
> senting us with ideas that at first seem
> extreme you draw more people away from the
> staunch conservative point of view and
> closer to accepting your ideas.

To which McKenna responds:

> Your question assumes a kind of rhetorical
> strategy on my part. I am aware of that the
> ideas are shocking to some, but they are not
> communicated with an intent to shock, their
> are communicated with the notion that they
> are the best approximation to the truth as I
> knew it. I do confess that narrow minds
> bring out a kind of reckless intellectual
> pranksterism in me. I remind you of J. B.
> S. Haldane's wonderful observation: "The
> world is not only stranger than we suppose,
> it is stranger than we *can* suppose." My
> faith in the power of novelty to transform
> the world is ... an uplifting realization

that I share in the hope that others' will
find as much pleasure in it as I have.

Finally, an example of a group of students challenging McKenna
more directly about the rhetorical difficulty of his text:

It is clear throughout your whole book that
language and communication have a strong
emphasis on meaning. But on page 93 you
state,

"This is a kind of Islamic paradise in which
one is free to experience all the pleasures
of the flesh provided one realizes that one
is a holographic projection of a solid-state
matrix that is microminiaturized, supercon-
ducting, and nowhere to be found; it is part
of the plenum."

It is ironic how you use vague and complicated wording to get your point across, In
a class of educated college students very
few could understand the depth of some of
your topics. Who is your target audience
and why?

McKenna responds by defending stylistic choice, but recognizing the
careful consideration reflected in the students' message:

Great question. Truthfully there is an
element of almost self parody in the statement that you quoted. It is partially intended to amuse. I like the taste and feel
of big words, I am a William Faulkner and
James Joyce kind of guy. Which doesn't mean
that I am intentionally obscure or difficult. I believe that people should exercise
their full capacity for vocabulary. Speech
is the one form of art that we all do every

```
day, why not make it complex, baroque and
beautiful as well as interesting and to the
point? William Blake said: "If the truth can
be told so as to be understood, it will be
believed." I am trying to tell the truth as
I know it, in a way so that it can be be-
lieved, but it is a complex truth and is
betrayed by simplification. Wish me luck.
All the best,
      Terence McKenna
```

We believe these examples demonstrate some of the tangible strengths of such an assignment. This last student message, particularly, demonstrates that as a result of the rhetorical situation provided by the e-mail correspondence with the author, students returned to the text with a more critical approach. In return, although McKenna did not respond directly to the question of his target audience, his response gives students a deeper level of understanding about his writing, causing them to consider stylistic and rhetorical needs in tandem.

One change the instructor feels he would make in this kind of exercise (depending of course on the time available, and the stamina of your participant) is to encourage a second round of questions. By asking students to follow up on a participant's answers, and asking a participant to send one more set of responses, students will obviously develop even more deeply their understanding of the topics at hand. If the participant has the time to offer, of course, the contact might be extended much longer than two sets of messages, increasing the benefits of the exercise in proportion to the number of exchanges.

Chapter Three
Have We Got Some
News For You: Usenet News

3

WHAT ARE USENET NEWSGROUPS? _____

"A place for everything, and everything in its place." And Usenet newsgroups have become an extremely popular place. Currently, there are more than six thousand newsgroups online, with an estimated three to four million Usenet users. Perhaps this popularity can be explained by the way that Usenet accommodates such a diversity of topics and individuals, containing groups as divergent as *alt.fan.rush-limbaugh*, *alt.sex.spanking*, *k12.ed.science*, *misc.activism.progressive*, and *soc.culture.kurdish*. Not only is there a place for everything, there's probably a place for everyone.

Newsgroups are similar to private bulletin boards and commercial message sites, but if you are teaching at an academic institution you will most likely be connected to Usenet, an enormous network of groups from sites around the world which have been collected and organized by a news server at your institution. In general, Usenet newsgroups are topic-specific sites where the "news" is a mixture of encoded multimedia, personal postings, carefully crafted articles, and conventional newsfeeds. The "groups" organized by the Usenet hierarchy not only distribute these topic-centered materials, but also fulfill an important social function by providing spaces where individuals can meet, interact and engage in discussion.

Key Terms

Flame: usually a pejorative term describing a post that attacks a message or an individual. A flame usually has a confrontational tone and offers little or no constructive criticism.

News Server: also known as "News Host." An Internet-connected server which organizes, stores and distributes newsgroup messages.

Newsfeed: messages posted to a newsgroup which originate from a wire service or other traditional news source.

Newsgroups: topic-centered sites devoted to discussion and to the exchange of articles, messages, or other media.

Newsreader: also known as a "news client." A program which provides an easy interface for reading, composing, posting and downloading newsgroup messages.

Post: to send an electronic message to a newsgroup. Also used as a noun to refer to the message itself.

Thread: a posting and a series of replies on the same topic, usually with the same subject heading.

Usenet: one subset of the Internet which facilitates the exchange of messages and discussion. Most colleges and universities are involved with Usenet groups rather than private or commercial bulletin boards. The broad classification of Usenet contains thousands of topic-centered newsgroups organized hierarchically by name.

Newsgroups can be directed at audiences ranging from the local to the international. Many academic institutions, for example, will offer newsgroup services for affiliated courses and individuals. Most groups, however, are global in scope. For the purposes of our discussion, we have divided groups roughly into three categories: newsfeeds, moderated groups, and unmoderated groups.

- **Newsfeeds** represent the most familiar form of newsgroup information. Groups based on newsfeeds collect traditional news sources from wire services like the Associated Press and Reuters. Usually listed under the large hierarchy of Clarinet or "Clari" newsgroups, these groups provide students doing basic research with instant access to a wide variety of current resources. Check with your systems administrator about the availability of the Clari newsfeeds at your institution.

- **Moderated groups** operate on the premise that messages posted to the group should be filtered through a moderator; therefore, not every message sent to a moderated list will be posted. Because messages which lean toward unsubstantiated personal rants are generally censored, postings to a moderated list often fall into the category of expert opinions or topic-centered articles. These posts are usually well argued and offer fairly knowledgeable insight into a research topic.

- **Unmoderated groups** are open to anyone and offer the best window for viewing the diverse types of written interaction that can take place on Usenet newsgroups. Messages display varying levels of formality (ranging between scholarly articles and "chat") and often prompt substantial interaction. A posted message and subsequent responses (comprising a "thread") reveal a dialogue which often moves between a series of arguments and counter-arguments.

While these categories represent useful distinctions, most newsgroup discussions are unmoderated and involve a range of activities and types of messages. In some ways, the messages found on a newsgroup can be compared to those shared via a listserv (see Chapter Two). The postings generally relate to a single topic and often provide insight and perspectives from knowledgeable individuals that can be easily incorporated as resources for student compositions. Some groups are more directly analogous to traditional print media, while others range toward personal opinion.

Throughout the rest of this chapter we will:

- look at the ways in which newsgroups involve us in a larger community, focusing attention on issues of audience;
- discuss in more detail the types of information available through newsgroups and examine the ways that these materials and activities foreground the need for critical reading and source evaluation;
- provide sample assignments and details about setting up, choosing and posting to newsgroups; and
- conclude with a case study demonstrating a research project that makes use of extensive newsgroup activity.

WHY USE USENET NEWSGROUPS?

Finding a Community

Thinking about each one of the thousands of newsgroups as a separate rhetorical situation—with its own unique subject matter, audience, and level of expertise required by the participant—is a helpful way to visualize the potential benefits of using newsgroups in the classroom. By providing an opportunity for students to communicate with a larger and more varied readership, newsgroups give students concrete examples of rhetorical situations in which different audiences demand different argumentative strategies. The feedback students receive from audiences outside the classroom helps shape their understanding of writing as a socially defined act and pushes them to focus on communicating ideas and exchanging information rather than simply making a grade on an English paper.

Much of what we said in the previous chapter about the ways e-mail constructs certain kinds of audiences and certain rhetorical situations applies to newsgroups as well. Confronting an audience that is not immediately present (and what's more, not familiar) forces students to appeal to that audience's sense of values and standards.

Although the audiences for newsgroup postings are quite broad, moving far beyond the range of a single instructor and a handful of peers, they are delimited in other ways, primarily by the topic of each of the newsgroups. On an active group, the feedback that students receive comes from informed readers who are knowledgeable about their subject matter—particularly beneficial when students are writing research papers covering a wide range of topics, some of which may be out of the area of expertise of the instructor. Students can post messages early in their research process to ask advice about sources or to get feedback on their ideas as they begin to take shape.

Using newsgroups, students can make important gains in their research (an idea developed more in the following section) and experience a "workshop" environment in which various rhetorical strategies can be tested. At the same time, students learn that statements which are poorly argued or expressed unclearly will often be challenged, critiqued or ignored by other readers. The inherently discursive situation of a newsgroup, in which writing can comfortably be used as a tool for dialogue, encourages a responsibility on the part of students to be aware of their audiences and to be conscious of the fact that clear writing is vital for effective communication.

Concerning the issue of audience (as well as the socio-economic issues of access to computer technology), we should note that a number of these newsgroups are in languages other than English. Students who have multilingual skills, therefore, are able to situate themselves in further discourse communities which may provide an especially interesting perspective on the work for a particular essay. Meanwhile, showing your class the content of newsgroups in languages other than English can lead to fruitful discussions about access to information itself. For example, the existence of a few non-English newsgroups points out the dominance of English overall, a fact which might otherwise be naturalized into the experience of using newsgroups, and go unnoticed. While pointing out the availability of a knowledgeable audience for certain issues, instructors should also stress the Internet's underrepresentation of certain minority groups, economic classes and even entire continents. Though we have suggested that newsgroups provide an expanded audience for your classroom, remember that a newsgroup audience may have important gaps in its demographic makeup.

Mining the Communal Resource

Newsgroups closely intertwine research and conversation. A student may begin by gleaning information from a newsgroup in a manner which resembles research, but soon may post queries for further information to the same newsgroup, or participate actively in the group's ongoing discussion. While this discussion can be beneficial for rhetorical reasons which we highlight throughout this chapter, if the student is using the discussion to clarify points about the topic of his writing, then the conversation itself can serve as a means of research.

Perhaps the greatest benefit of researching with newsgroups is their currency. One type of group offers newsfeeds from wire services like the Associated Press and Reuters, providing materials which appear in newspapers around the country. News is thus available to students with the immediacy that they expect from reading the paper or watching television, with the additional strength of near comprehensive coverage—anything the wire services produce is available online, whereas any particular newspaper has to radically curtail the amount of material it is able to present.

```
┌─────────────────────────────────────────────────────────┬────────┐
│                  Full Group List                         │        │
├──────────────┬──────────────────────────────────────────┴────────┤
│ alt.creative │▤□▤▤▤ Third World Newsgroups ▤                      │
│ alt.cuddle   │                                                    │
│ alt.cult-movie│6289  alt.activism                                 │
│ alt.cult-movie│ 491  alt.activism.d                               │
│ alt.cult-movie│  17  alt.culture.somalia                          │
│ alt.culture.a│      alt.culture.tamil                             │
│ alt.culture.ar│  5   alt.culture.southasianet                     │
│ alt.culture.au│ 66   clari.news.poverty                           │
│ alt.culture.be│322   clari.news.terrorism                         │
│ alt.culture.bu│448   clari.news.usa.gov.foreign_pol               │
│ alt.culture.cd│548   clari.world.africa                           │
│ alt.culture.eg│ 87   clari.world.africa.south_afric               │
│ alt.culture.el│      clari.world.americas                         │
│ alt.culture.hd│108   clari.world.americas.caribbean               │
│ alt.culture.ir│ 48   clari.world.americas.central                 │
│ alt.culture.ir│ 86   clari.world.americas.mexico                  │
│ alt.culture.kd│268   clari.world.americas.south                   │
│ alt.culture.ke│      clari.world.asia                             │
│ alt.culture.ku│ 72   clari.world.asia.central                     │
│ alt.culture.mi│192   clari.world.asia.india                       │
│ alt.culture.ne│204   clari.world.asia.south                       │
│ alt.culture.nu│567   clari.world.asia.southeast                   │
│ alt.culture.or│124   clari.world.mideast.iran                     │
│ alt.culture.ri│ 27   clari.world.mideast.iraq                     │
│ alt.culture.sd│352   misc.activism.progressive                    │
│ alt.culture.sd│ 34   clari.world.mideast.turkey                   │
│ alt.culture.sd│9999  soc.culture.indian                           │
└──────────────┴────────────────────────────────────────────────────┘
```

A list of "third world" newsgroups set up for a composition course

Although we have outlined distinctions between newsfeeds, moderated and unmoderated groups, perhaps a more valuable taxonomy classifies groups according to the nature of their messages and conversations. Besides newsfeeds, these groups fall roughly into two categories: "serious" and "chat." The serious newsgroups may be moderated or unmoderated, but are distinguished by the fact that they are more analytical and present a wider variety of opinions than the wire service groups. Participants in these groups are often experts, and (particularly with the active participation of members of

47

the academic community) their opinions are often based on careful research of their own.

One of the benefits of these newsgroups is that they offer a significant amount of alternative information (especially concerning international and "third world" issues) that is often absent from mainstream news sources. For example, along with international newsfeeds on the January 1994 uprising in Chiapas, Mexico, newsgroups have provided the text of political pamphlets from the region which were scanned and posted to the net. Thus, current, locally produced information (unfiltered by the political investments of publishers) becomes available to interested readers around the world.

A third set of groups, probably the least useful in an academic setting, might be described as social message boards which focus on nonacademic subjects. Your students will have access to groups like *alt.sex.stories*, *alt.alien.vampire.flonk.flonk.flonk*, and *rec.games. video.arcade* that will probably not be appropriate for your class. These groups can be distracting and instructors should take measures to ensure that the class does not deteriorate into reckless flonking. While you will likely want students to avoid these most extreme groups which have questionable pedagogical value, there are a number of "chat" groups which can be useful for your class. For example, the conversation on *alt.fan.tarantino* would prove interesting if the class had watched the film *Reservoir Dogs*. Although their topics may be less serious than either of the two types of groups discussed above, instructors can use these groups pedagogically, for instance to demonstrate the poor ethos of a flame, or to discuss the conversational nature of newsgroups in general.

Reading Critically

The volume of information available on newsgroups highlights the need for a pedagogy that stresses evaluation and critical reading skills. Because of the comparative absence of filtering processes like those more broadly employed in print publication, excellent materials are "published" on Usenet which would otherwise only find space in small, low circulation presses, or in local distribution situations, if anywhere. At the same time, because anyone with access to the Internet can post information and arguments to newsgroups, the material can often be problematic for student research papers. This disparity in the quality of information that is available provides excellent opportunities for teaching evaluation skills and demands that students read sources critically rather than blindly insert information into their work.

In some senses newsgroups constitute a paradox—a source of information which can be seen as both less reliable and more reliable than familiar items such as journal articles. The sense in which they may be less reliable is clear. Students just beginning to learn how to use sources effectively in their research often relegate a certain authority to the written word. Hastily written flames present students with "published" sources that may or may not provide them with viable arguments, accurate information, or effective rhetorical models. Contrasting this type of potentially problematic message are the two other broad categories of messages discussed above: postings from newsfeeds and messages from the "serious," more analytical discussion groups (which often make use of detailed research).

What is significant about Usenet is that in the majority of groups there is little distinction made between all these various types of messages, a distinction print maintains much more rigidly by marginalizing less "authoritative" responses. As a result, newsgroups take on a kind of rhetorical reliability which is quite different from that surrounding the printed source. When a user enters a thread of discussion in a newsgroup, she is instantly surrounded by a number of divergent voices and opinions, all pulling against one another in a variety of ways. Through a careful process of critical reading, this user might actually come to a more reliable sense of the full complexity of an issue than she might reach after reading isolated printed sources. The printed text by its very singular authority often cannot acknowledge the full range of other positions and voices which surround it in a public debate. Reading newsgroups, however, one gets the sense that even if all the users are hackers, or hacks, or both, we must appreciate the extent to which even hacks help define the terminology of a debate, its boundaries, its stakes.

```
 -          William Wallis      Re: More news on Foster
 -          Children Now        Chidren Now:   New Web Si
▽  7        Jim Nakamura        Re: What Happened to Hea
            Donna Kinney        Re: What Happened to Hea
            Karl Dussik         Re: What Happened to Hea
            Jim Nakamura        Re: What Happened to Hea
            Jim Nakamura        Re: What Happened to Hea
            Sandy               Re: What Happened to Hea
            ir0002120interra    Re: What Happened to Hea
 -          Jon Roland          Re: REPORT: A.D.L. of B'
▷  2        Pete Zakel          Re: MEDICAL POT MEANS PO
 -          Kevin Darcy         Re: What will support@ne
▷  4        Ted Krueger         Re: Ok, but what about r
```

A thread discussing health care in alt.activism

In general, newsgroups facilitate the process of gathering various perspectives on the same issue. Messages found within the same thread often comment on, critique and/or revise previous messages. The thread presents rich material to demonstrate the fundamentals of critical reading—that is, granting the writer as much credibility as possible while simultaneously keeping in mind opposing points of view and possible points of rebuttal. Instead of giving students a single article on an issue, or two pieces which oppose one another, instructors might suggest students look at an entire thread in a newsgroup. By working with the thread as a unit, instructors can demonstrate that any position will be open to refutation and that a successful argument depends upon the writer's ability to place divergent perspectives into conversation.

HOW CAN YOUR CLASS USE NEWSGROUPS?_____

Accessing the Local Community

We have already seen in Chapter Two how a class listserv or nick-name file in e-mail can provide numerous advantages for communicating within a class or between sections of a course. Similarly, a class newsgroup offers instructors and students a place outside of the classroom in which to engage in conversation about the course. Whereas the class listserv is invaluable for conducting the daily operations of course management (sending notices to students, forwarding pertinent readings, making changes in assignments, etc.), often a local class newsgroup (for one or more sections) produces more substantial and engaging discussion about the course.

Although setting up a local Usenet newsgroup for a class is generally a fairly simple procedure, the specifics of the process will probably vary from site to site. Contact your systems administrator to find out what policies your institution follows for creating local groups and if you as an instructor will be able to create your own class group.

If you can set up a newsgroup, you will be faced with the task of effectively integrating it into your classroom practice. The class newsgroup will almost certainly assume different roles in the classroom depending upon the nature of the course, the teaching style of the instructor, and the structure of the syllabus. Many instructors simply set up a group, teach the students how to post to it, and allow the group to operate with relatively little supervision. This method can produce lively discussions, especially for students who have experience posting to newsgroups and who are comfortable with the medium. However, we have often found that without direction, students unfamiliar with newsgroups will simply ignore the class group and most of the conversation will be carried on by only a few eager participants.

51

We have also tried in the past to incorporate the class newsgroup very rigorously into our course syllabi. Not only did we ask students to engage in conversation with one another, we also required them to post shorter papers and journal-like assignments to the group. There are several advantages to utilizing the class group in this way:

- Instructors can use the newsgroup as an easily accessible storage place for student papers and assignments so that a system of peer editing can be set up in the newsgroup itself.
- A group which contains substantial student writing assignments can serve as a forum for displaying student work to other instructors and the local Internet community, and can ultimately be archived as a significant set of materials tracing the written production of a given class.
- A group like this can also serve as a model for the type of Usenet newsgroup which contains important documents rather than just "chat" or conversation.

This last "advantage" of the closely-moderated newsgroup, however, can also lead to some less productive dynamics within it. A class group where students are required to post significant elements of their coursework runs the risk of becoming something of a "data dump." Although assigning postings makes a class group an integral part of the course, doing so tends to discourage dialogue and interaction between students. Because of the time and effort involved in reading through even one three-page paper, let alone twenty-two of them, students come to see the newsgroup as a place to turn in assignments rather than a place to discuss the ways in which those assignments are making them think. A number of our students, in fact, felt that in this regard, our class group had become unlike other newsgroups they frequented. Since the students were unlikely to read through all of their peers' work unless required, we ultimately came to see this type of class newsgroup as a resource which was interesting and important for instructors, but much less viable for students.

Newsgroups in the Classroom: Step-by-Step

1. Well before the start of the school term, explore the availability of newsgroups at your institution: does it sponsor its own news server? does it subscribe to the "Clari" family of newsfeeds? does it offer you the capability to create your own newsgroup for course use?

2. Early in the term, introduce your students to the newsreader they will be using.

3. Compile and distribute to your students a list of newsgroups related to the themes of your course. If your students are using a workstation client newsreader, this list can be distributed to them as a file readable by the client.

4. Familiarize your students with the different types of newsgroups and the material available on them (see p. 43). Consider giving them an assignment to follow and analyze the discussion on one or more groups.

5. Encourage your students to devote a diskette solely to newsgroup research. Explain to them the currency and ephemeral nature of newsgroup postings, and the need to save useful materials as soon as they are found.

6. Establish a newsgroup of your own for class use, if desired. Remember a newsgroup has the distribution capabilities of a listserv, but the postings are stored in a central location and can be accessed by a wider audience than the subscribers to a list.

7. To make students responsible for participating in the class newsgroup, yet give them some flexibility in the manner of their participation, consider establishing a portfolio system to grade newsgroup postings. Collect these portfolios serval times during the semester to encourage consistent activity on the newsgroup.

A final method instructors might use to incorporate a class group into their syllabi (and one which has proven to be particularly effective for our classes) offers something of a compromise between giving students total freedom in their posting and requiring them to post a specific number of completed assignments. Since many students will choose not to participate in the group if instructors make postings optional, requiring students to send messages to the class group may be necessary. Instead of assigning specific dates and topics for student posts, however, we have recently begun giving students complete autonomy in their decisions about when and what they choose to post to the group.

Students are free to post any comments, questions, suggestions or other messages to the group as long as they are related to the course. We also try to encourage students to reply to existing messages so that threads of conversation build up and students interact and engage with each other. An instructor can choose either to participate actively in the discussions or to "lurk." Our experience suggests that class newsgroups which let students direct the conversation produce some engaging discussions and contribute tremendously to the course.

The evaluation of student newsgroup postings presents yet another quandary for instructors. With no form of evaluation it is very difficult to ensure that your students are consistently participating in the newsgroups. However, grading the posts may discourage "spontaneous" dialogue. With a grade in the balance, we have found that students almost inevitably produce work which attempts to comply to the standards of academic prose, rather than engage in the more informal writing and conversational style that is characteristic of newsgroup messages.

Instructors who seek a middle ground between a stilted formality and a more natural conversation in student messages may want to consider establishing a portfolio system of evaluation. Writing portfolios provide a flexible means of keeping track of and evaluating student posts, while allowing students to converse without feeling like their grade depends upon every word they write. We suggest implementing some sort of portfolio for informal assignments which could include the best student newsgroup posts—perhaps specifying that you are looking for those posts with substantial analytical content. If you collect these portfolios several times during the semester, you can make sure your students begin posting to the group early and maintain that momentum throughout the course.

Once students feel comfortable posting on a class list, they often begin frequenting other Usenet newsgroups. Instructors might consider allowing students to include in their writing portfolios posts they make to other groups. You might even encourage students to put their writing into practice by engaging in conversations about issues which are important to them whether or not they pertain to the course. For example, one of us had a Taiwanese student who became very involved in a newsgroup that dealt with issues facing Taiwanese-Americans. Because he was deeply invested in the group's discussion, he posted numerous messages, raised questions and argued positions. This type of writing, although certainly less formal than that produced for a graded essay assignment, still involves principles of argumentation fundamental to a composition class. These personal postings also provide students with meaningful issues to discuss and, perhaps, a more comfortable forum in which to address an audience generally more interested in dialogue than in judgment.

Posting and Gathering

With literally thousands of different Usenet groups to choose from, there is an excellent chance that your students will discover groups discussing issues which are important to them, and/or which will be useful for researching class projects. At the same time, however, the overwhelming list of groups can be disorienting, and the process of searching through thousands of prefixed and suffixed names can be frustrating and time-consuming for both students and instructors. Along with setting up a local class group, then, we strongly recommend that instructors use their newsreaders to set up a list of relevant groups. For most newsreaders this will mean "subscribing" to or selecting the individual groups that you want the class to receive. Obviously, you will not be able to predict all of the individual interests of your students—suggest to them that they scan through the full list on their own—but by setting up a list of anywhere between ten and two hundred groups, you will give your students a manageable set of resources. They can then begin to see the range of different groups and types of conversation available in Usenet news.

 **Newsreaders and Servers**

- The most basic newsreading option is a client program residing on a remote Internet-connected machine. By Telnetting to an Internet account and activating a newsreading client, a user can read and respond to newsgroup messages.

- A more user-friendly form of newsreader operates from the machines of individual users. These workstation clients allow users to customize lists of groups and offer searching, decoding and other capabilities.

- Most World Wide Web browsers now incorporate newsreading interfaces into their operations (see Chapter Five). Like workstation newsreaders, they coordinate the reading and composition of messages.

(See Appendix Five for more client/server information.)

We highly recommend that you get your students accustomed to the idea of browsing newsgroups as a means of gathering materials for their research papers and projects. There are a number of topics for which Usenet will offer more (and more significant) materials than a traditional library. Students who use Usenet groups to research extremely current topics, or topics which are particularly heavily represented online—current "third world" issues, environmental concerns, computer or technology-related topics—will very likely find much more material than they would searching through a library's collection of books and periodicals.

Also remember that newsgroups offer an extremely broad array of materials. Not only will students be able to find well-written articles on their topics, but they will also generally run across important documents (for example, government legislation or official UN statements), as well as an array of opinions and perspectives on the issue. As we suggested above, this variety of information and multiplicity of voices can be addressed in a unit on incorporating and evaluating source materials. The Case Study at the end of this chapter provides an example of the type of work students can produce when they effectively utilize the resources available on Usenet News.

Instructors should make their students aware that newsgroups, by their very nature, are geared towards researching current events. Since the groups have limited storage size, newer postings displace older ones after a certain amount of time or after the group has exceeded its size limitations. For researchers this means that the content of the groups is constantly changing, and a post which is available one week may be gone the next (especially on groups with heavy traffic). Instructors should remind students, then, to always save and document any news posts that they find particularly useful. We generally have students reserve a diskette solely for their newsgroup work and try to stress that "too much is better than not enough" when gathering information from Usenet. When using client software (see Appendix Five for a short list of newsreaders), students can archive the material they find online and easily "cut and paste" quotations into their papers once they have begun the composition process. This will ensure that their sources will not disappear before they have a chance to get needed statistics or citation information (see Appendix Three for citation information).

Additionally, when assigning a research paper which relies heavily on newsgroup sources, we encourage you to utilize the interactive capabilities of the groups. Beyond just mining Usenet for existing resources, students should be encouraged to post questions and requests for information about their topic to appropriate newsgroups.

Usenet provides a tremendous amount of expertise on even the most obscure topics. Remind your students, though, that the people reading and writing these groups are not librarians paid to answer questions—they participate in the discussions for their own benefit and enjoyment. Students should avoid making group members feel obligated to answer obvious factual or historical questions. Recommend that students spend time familiarizing themselves with the key issues, terms, and players in a debate before posting questions to the groups.

This is not to say that the newsgroup audience is unwilling to offer assistance. In fact, participants are surprisingly helpful and will often write long and thoughtful replies to student requests. In order to receive this help, though, students will have to spend time carefully composing their questions. A confident but polite ethos will go a long way towards eliciting useful feedback, but will not make up for a poorly conceived message. The best questions will spark debate on the group and allow the group members to offer assistance to the student while maintaining their existing level of conversation. If your students make the effort to compose informed, detailed requests, we think both they and you will be pleased with the response.

Introductory Exercises: Newsgroups

• Select a newsgroup related to a course topic and assign students the task of following its discussion, working through basic newsreading skills: locating the group, scanning and reading messages, downloading information to a diskette, and finally posting messages to the group. • As students become familiar with the availability and organization of information on Usenet, have them prepare a short annotated list of newsgroups related to a research topic or a combination of personal and school-related interest. • Create a newsgroup, utilizing it like a listserv for the course (but encourage students to consider the wider audiences that newsgroups facilitate). Develop threads of discussion by assigning students the responsibility both of posting new messages and commenting on previous ones (consider a portfolio system to grade newsgroup postings).

Sample Assignments

- Pull 4-8 postings about the same issue (particularly an issue not getting much coverage in the mainstream press) from a variety of groups to show the different types of information available on newsgroups. Make sure to include sources which would traditionally seem credible (such as newsfeeds or more "academic" articles) along with some posts which might appear to carry less authority (for instance, several posts from a thread of discussion). Have your class evaluate the sources for use in a hypothetical research paper. Stress that nontraditional sources can be incorporated as well as more scholarly pieces, and highlight the ways that news, both online and from the mainstream media, must be read critically and evaluated from an informed perspective.

- Have each student in your class follow the conversations on a newsgroup for several days. After observing the group, have them write up a short description of the types of messages that are posted, the apparent purpose of the group, and the audience to which it seems most directed. Have students do a rhetorical analysis of one or two representative postings to illustrate their description of the group's function and audience.

- After having students do some initial research on a subject, ask them to post a request for information to a set of selected newsgroups. Make sure that students write thoughtful questions or comments, keeping in mind the expertise of the group's audience. Well-written inquiries about specific topics or issues will generally bring good responses, whereas awkward, overly generalized questions are more likely to meet with apathy or even hostility.

NEWSGROUP CASE STUDY: THIRD WORLD NEWS AND CLASSROOM DEVELOPMENT

E306 Rhetoric and Composition
Instructor: Bill Paredes-Holt

This case study comes from an assignment developed over three semesters by Bret Benjamin (and revised and taught by Benjamin, Bill Paredes-Holt, and Jean Lee Cole). The assignments below are part of a larger process that teaches first-year composition students to write a knowledgeable and well-researched ethical argument about a particular problem facing a "third world" country. In particular, we wanted students to understand their position as relatively privileged authors of the first world, and to assess how that privilege shaped the way their writing would be seen by a larger audience. A significant part of the assignment was to realize the complexity of the issues at hand. The examples here are taken from the summer of 1994, during which time the United States' relationships with Bosnia-Herzogovina, Rwanda, and Haiti were all coming to a boil. The research paper assignment follows:

> You will write a 6-8 page argumentative
> essay about the position of the "first
> world" in relation to the "third world."
> Your essay can examine a particular aspect
> of US or European foreign policy (military
> intervention, foreign ownership, economic
> aid for particular projects or regimes,
> etc.), or it can look more generally at
> issues that face the "third world" as an
> imaginary whole (environmental concerns,
> health, population control, etc.). In ei-
> ther case, I would prefer that you focus on
> a single country so that you will have con-
> crete evidence and examples to ground your
> argument in the specific local conditions of
> a particular geographic site.

> Ethical arguments, perhaps more than any
> other, force writers to interrogate the
> assumptions that validate their explicit
> claims and reasons. Creating an argument
> based on research about topics such as the
> ones above will require you to make tough
> choices and compromises. Remember that you
> should not simply present information about
> a given situation, but also make an ethical
> evaluation of the situation and present a
> course of action.

In this assignment, newsgroups served two main functions: giving students an audience for which to shape their ideas, and providing a resource to draw upon for further information. In addition to using the class newsgroup to coordinate with their research partners, to practice posting to newsgroups, and to receive peer critiques, students were required to gather sources from newsgroups and to post questions and comments to relevant groups. This assignment included a substantial amount of research from both traditional library and computer-based sources, but newsgroups were central to the project.

Instructors compiled a list of about 200 "third world" newsgroups like *alt.activism*, *soc.culture.african*, *misc.activism.progressive*, *soc.culture.mexican*, and *clari.news.refugees*. Initially, students were asked to browse for topics they found interesting, follow the threads of conversation, and look for other postings that dealt with the same topic, all in hopes of finding a provocative and usable topic for their final papers. By browsing these diverse newsgroups, students entered the newsgroup conversation, and began building a bibliography by saving interesting posts to their diskettes. They used all types of postings generally found in newsgroups: newsfeeds, article-length posts, and alerts distributed by activist organizations, as well as more personally oriented opinion pieces.

Students developed their projects in stages. They began by posting possible topics to the class newsgroup, *utexas.class.e306*, in order to find research partners. After finding partners, the students began preliminary research in the library, building a bibliography first from encyclopedias and general reference books and then moving on to articles and book chapters. Each then posted a brief message giving a history of their topic country and a second message which defined the problem that they would explore. As part of this development, students wrote peer critiques of each other's definitions, concentrating especially on how to frame the problem for a larger audience and how to provide relevant background information. At the same time, students were responsible for keeping up with the "third world" newsgroups; these groups provided a continuous source of material and a provocative forum for discussion.

Next, students were asked to post a message to one of the unmoderated newsgroups that they had been following. The students were asked to fit their posts into a thread of conversation in the newsgroup, either by responding to a post and explaining how the original post fit into their understanding of the subject (and thus in the process accommodating, refuting, or asking for clarification), or by deciding how much of their own position they needed to explain in order to generate responses and open up a new avenue of discussion.

By posting to an outside newsgroup, the instructors hoped that their students would think about presenting their arguments to a large, well-informed audience and use their own ideas and research to enter into a conversation. In addition, the instructors wanted them to receive useful new ideas or information from the group. Though the quality of the responses varied, almost all students received responses containing either critiques of their arguments or suggestions for further reading.

For example, a number of students who posted to the newsgroup *soc.culture.bosnia-herzogovina* found out how vital the conflict in Bosnia is to some people. Besides initiating long threads in which different sides in the newsgroups began responding to each other, the students could see how ethnic Serbs, Muslims, Croats, and other participants in the US, France, Great Britain, and Australia responded to student posts on the subject.

One student, who posted under his nickname "Muhammad," supported intervention in Bosnia. His posting tried to question the ethics of a position which seemed to condone the ongoing slaughter. In a somewhat hasty post to the newsgroup, however, Muhammad's uncritical assumptions about the situation surfaced.

```
What is going on here.  Why is everyone so
against not helping Bosnia.  So are we going
to let the Muslims be killed of by those
gready ass Serbs and Croatians.  I'm not
saying go in and destroy every gun.just make
it fair.  The Serbs are stedly getting weap-
ons and supplies from Serbia who is helping
the Muslims.  Then we can help them with the
peace process.  Give them what they want.
If they want to be divided on ethnic lines
lets help them do that so we can get out as
quick as possible. Because no matter what,we
will always be involed while the conflict
still occurs.  Please someone leftwith a
good heart agree with me I know yall are out
there.
```

This post generated a response from one regular of the newsgroup who had posted constructive replies to a number of other student messages. In this case, though, the respondent took offense at the misrepresentation of Muslim/Croat relations. Deciphering at least one piece of the student's murky prose, the following passage answers Muhammad's question, "Who is helping the Muslims"?

```
Actually Croats you bloody idiot. Before the
war in Bosnia begun, Muslims received huge
quantities of arms from CROATIA and
```

CROATIANS (who according to you want to kill
muslims). Those quantities of arms continued
after the conflict between Croats and Muslims ended. I did not see you stinking
muslim countries providing arms.

Also don't dare forget you peace-of-no-good-
trash that during the war in Croatia (1991/
2), there were several thousands of MUSLIM
volunteers in Serb ranks going to Croatia
and killing Croats in Croatia for the benefit of Serbs. Bosnian president at that
time opposed any recognition of Croatia as
an independent state. If you want to talk
about crimes, chew on that.

Got that?

After receiving the flame, the student was forced to realize the misunderstandings that his writing produced. Because the student's nickname was Muhammad, the Croat on the newsgroup incorrectly identified the student's religious/ethnic affiliations, aligning him with the
"stinking Muslim countries." The student's poor choice of words and
unclear prose amplified the impression that he was hostile to Croats.
The respondent's spleen, though irresponsible in its own right, was
generated out of these misunderstandings and drew upon the strained
relations between Croats and Muslims in the area (only barely united
against the larger threat of the Serbs).

The hostility of this response emphasizes the importance of responsible student writing on newsgroups.   It highlights the need for
students to take their writing seriously and to consider how their
words will be received by an audience. This student had not realized
how even his nickname could be interpreted as a marker of a political position in the context of the ethnic conflict in Bosnia. He had
also unknowingly alienated this potentially hostile audience by refer-
ring to Croats as "Croatians," indicating to the reader his lack of
respect for the group of people and poor knowledge of the terms of

the discussion. This perception was compounded by the student's misconception that the Croats were helping the Serbs destroy the Muslims. Given the fact that the most recent aid to Muslims was given almost exclusively by Croats, the weight of these insults proved too much to bear. Although the flame was initially troubling to the student, it was ultimately a learning experience. Besides correcting his terminology (using "Croats" instead of "Croatians"), Muhammad was able to express in his paper a more accurate understanding of the complicated divisions and allegiances which characterize the ethnic/national conflicts in Bosnia-Herzogovina.

The next example illustrates how a student might incorporate newsgroup interaction into a research paper.

One of the richest exchanges that took place during the course of the assignment occurred between a student and a number of South Africans on the topic of the effectiveness of US led economic sanctions during apartheid. The following is the original post by our student.

```
I have recently done research on the disman-
tling of apartheid in South Africa.  There
were many contributing factors to the end of
apartheid including U.S. pressure on the
South African government through economic
sanctions and trade embargoes. There were
mixed feelings about whether the sanctions
would be worth the negative effects they
would have.  The sanctions put thousands of
black people out of work in South Africa
forcing them into lives of poverty.
        Some people felt that economic sanc-
tions and a U. S. pullout should not be
used.  Instead, they proposed more busi-
nesses should be brought into South Africa
with the thought process that more educated
blacks in South Africa would eventually
produce political empowerment for them.  My
```

feeling on this stance is that this would be
a very lengthy process that would still not
insure the end of apartheid completely.

Others felt that the sanctions
should be less strict so that the effects
would less harmful to South African workers.
I feel that nothing short of the strongest
possible actions could have pressured the
stubborn South African government into the
termination of apartheid. Although there
have been many hard hit by the sanctions,
the process, in my opinion went as fast as
it possibly could because of the U.S. pressures. After all, South Africa is now becoming a democratic government and the U.S.
has plans to provide aid to those hard hit
families.

I would like some opinions on this
subject if anyone is interested.

As you can see, the student wrote the post carefully, outlining his
position and clearly explaining the limitations of the other positions
he has seen. This post generated a thoughtful and helpful response
from a South African citizen the next day:

Interesting and *tough* question.
FWIW, I don't think yr the only one who's
debated the topic down the years and, like
as not, there's no perfect answer or abso-
lutes (ideological blinkers notwithstand-
ing).

Some basic facts to perhaps vector
in.....
1. The SA economy has not grown in significantly in real terms since the economic
fallout from the *ancient* 1973 Oil Crisis.
There were, I think, a coupla yrs ('80-81)
when there was some marginal real growth,
but that was all. Today, everyone gets

jolly if annual growth hits 2.5 or 3%. Note
that this trend fully predates the early-
mid-1980's disinvestment-sanctions pattern.

2. Black economic "empowerment" began to
take shape in the early 1970's (the Durban
textile strikes of '73 as an e.g.) — this
lead to the formation of Black unions culmi-
nating in the Weihan report of '79 which, in
turn, set the trend for explosive growth in
this area thru the 1980's. (Note that over-
seas owned firms were the organisations
which first established and encouraged the
Black union movement — Smith & Nephew in
Durban being, I think, the first.

3. Large scale sanctions and disinvestment
took off in the mid-1980's and, given a
degree of lag-effect, perhaps became a no-
table *influence* by (say) '87-88.

4. '89 saw the introduction of more strin-
gent monetary policy to bring down infla-
tion. This was naturally deflationary — the
intervening 4-odd years have seen no real
change in this area.

   Opinion time, in the light of the
above facts...... the SA economy was in a
rather fragile state for perhaps 10 yrs
prior to the introduction of sanctions\
disinvestment. Sanctions policies would
thus seem to have worsened the situation and
made its improvement more difficult, but
not IMO directly caused it. In sum, they
were an *influence* and it is thus a error
to hold that there was some linear
relationship(s) of cause and effect at work.

This message was read and critiqued by another South African citizen, whose message was in turn answered by the first South African with clarification. In addition, one reader of the newsgroup responded via e-mail and kept up a correspondence with the student for a number of days. These different conversations fostered a much more complex presentation of the issues, an understanding of the interrelatedness of events, and the difficulty of making simple claims about complex problems.

By making use of newsgroup correspondence, the student's paper was able to anticipate the arguments of opponents who said the sanctions would hurt the black community most and who favored sponsoring different types of economic growth:

```
The opponents were basically arguing that
sanctions would hurt the poor.  These argu-
ments could have worked, but they did not
realize that the South African economy had
featured poverty and maldistribution of
wealth long before sanctions.  "The South
African economy was in a rather fragile
state for about 10 years prior to the intro-
duction of sanctions....The South African
economy has not grown significantly since
the economic fallout from the 1973 oil cri-
sis.  Sanctions policies would thus seem to
have worsened the situation and made its
improvement more difficult, but not directly
caused it" (Author 1).  In sum, the sanc-
tions were meant to "influence" the South
African government into ending apartheid by
continuing South Africa's problems.
```

In addition to the materials gathered from the ClariNet group newsfeeds and moderated groups like *misc.activism.progressive*, this example shows exactly how correspondence in newsgroups can make students much more informed about their writing and eventually work the correspondence into their formal papers as a citation. Even if some students didn't get "useful" responses to their posts—ones that they could immediately quote from and put in their bibliography—they all had to adjust their writing and their arguments for a larger audience.

Chapter Four
Real-Time Discussion
and Textual Realities:
IRCs and MU*s

4

In this chapter we examine some of the ways that instructors can utilize IRCs and MU* spaces in their courses, and chart a broad progression which moves through real-time conversation, interaction, and composition. We feel that this progression serves not only as a useful chronology for introducing students to IRC and MU* basics, but also as a way to think pedagogically about working with these two technologies in successful ways.

 Key Terms

Channel: also referred to as a "line." An IRC channel is roughly equivalent to a C.B. radio frequency. Users join a channel to participate in the discussion that takes place among people logged on to that frequency.

Emote: to virtually represent an action during the real-time conversations on IRCs and MU*s. For example, a user named Socrates could type `":listens intently."` and the text transmitted to other participants would read `"Socrates listens intently."`

IRC (Internet Relay Chat): a system of Internet protocols and programs which allow users to participate on topic-centered, real-time discussion channels.

IRC Client: a program which provides an easy interface for a user who is logged on to an IRC channel.

MUDs (also MUSHes, Tiny MUSHes, MOOs, etc.): text-based virtual spaces ("Multi User Dungeons" or "Domains") which allow users to interact in real-time with other users or with the textual environment. The different acronyms refer to different protocols which perform similar functions.

Real-time: refers to the almost instantaneous transfer of messages in IRCs and MU*s, allowing users to communicate in a way which resembles synchronous face-to-face conversation. Real-time can be seen in opposition to e-mail and newsgroup messages, which are asynchronous.

WHAT ARE IRCS AND MU*S? _____

Internet Relay Chat (IRC)

The Internet Relay Chat (IRC) lines are the Internet's rough equivalent to a conference call or a C.B. radio channel. Like the Usenet groups discussed in the previous chapter, IRCs are topic-centered discussion areas. In IRCs, however, not only can users participate on an existing "channel," they can also quickly create their own. What makes IRCs interesting from a pedagogical perspective is that they allow real-time conversations to occur between multiple users from any number of sites around the globe. By "real-time" we mean that there is only a negligible lag-time between exchanges made by users on different computers. So, unlike e-mail or newsgroups, where there is an expected delay between messages which are more self-contained, IRC lines allow for synchronous conversation. Characters can also "emote," or describe actions which they are virtually "performing." For example, a user might "gracefully mount her soapbox" before launching into an extended remark. In this way users can interact through writing—not only with conversational dialogue, but also by contextualizing that dialogue with descriptive emotes.

A helpful way of looking at real-time discussions is as a hybrid that blends elements of written language with orality. A discussion in an IRC reads a little like a manuscript of a play in which a scrolling screen displays participants' names followed by a colon and then their dialogue or emotes. This sense of the theatrical is compounded by the fact that users are referred to as characters and they often take on pseudonyms while online. Like theater, which requires analysis of both the text and the performance, real-time interaction focuses attention on rhetorical issues arising at the intersection of writing and speech.

MU*s

The term MU* indicates a certain type of text-based, virtual environment, the first of which were the Multi User Domains (or "Dungeons"). MUDs were initially designed as a more sophisticated medium in which to engage in role-playing games like Dungeons and Dragons. Rather than use graphics to represent the fantastic worlds of these games, MUD participants could construct complex environments out of descriptive passages of text. These descriptions were placed on the Internet and scripted in a way which allowed multiple users to log on and be simultaneously present in the virtual space, adding an important interactive element to the games. Until recently these spaces have existed mainly as a forum for social interaction and gamesmanship. During the last few years, however, academics have started to see the value of these text-based environments and have begun to apply them to any number of scholarly projects.

MUDs gave birth to numerous different formats with names like MUSH and Tiny MUSH, each of which has slightly different protocols and scripting languages, as well as to the "MUD Object Oriented," or MOO. Rather than try to distinguish between MUDs, MUSHes, MOOs, and a host of other acronyms, we will use the term MU* to indicate a variety of these text-based virtual spaces. Because of the growing tendency for the more "academically oriented" of these spaces to be constructed using MOO scripts, we will provide examples mainly about MOO commands. Those details which do apply specifically to MOOs, however, can almost always be adapted with only minor variations to the other MU* formats.

Like the IRC channels, MU* protocols offer spaces in which real-time written conversation and interaction can take place. Unlike the IRCs, however, the space of a MU* is a highly circumscribed environment in which the surroundings will dictate many of the user's options. Within the same MU*, a user could easily wander into and out of the reference section of a university library, a public hearing in a fourth century BCE Grecian polis, a sci-fi nightmare, the second act of a Beckett play, the set of a movie, or just about anywhere else that someone might have imagined—all mapped out through textual descriptions. Rather than simply reading through the scrolling dialogue of an IRC channel, MU* users can move around, look at objects, and engage with their environment on a number of other levels.

As the above examples suggest, MU*s offer a writing class any number of possibilities for conversation and interaction. Students can, for example, visit online writing centers for help with their papers, attend online office hours from their home or dorm, role-play literary personas to explore elements of characterization, or learn about historical eras. MU*s also offer unique opportunities for student composition. Users can textually construct rooms, objects and spaces in MU*s. These activities provide the rhetoric and composition classroom with productive examples which help demonstrate the need to consider audience, organization, tone, style, and technique in descriptive writing.

In the remainder of this chapter we will continue to investigate real-time conversation, emoting and interacting with other users, engaging with an existing text-based environment, and ultimately constructing MU* spaces. Within these stages we will discuss the potential pedagogical value of both IRCs and MU*s, look at the practical uses and limitations of these technologies, and offer suggestions about using these tools. Finally, our Case Study looks at a set of student projects which use MU* spaces to present research about the effects of technology on socio-political aspects of culture.

WHY USE IRCS AND MU*S?

The Immediacy of Conversation

Since most computer-assisted classrooms offer programs that facilitate synchronous electronic communication, many instructors may be familiar with real-time interaction as it takes place on a local area network. If you don't have access to these functions locally, or if you wish to extend these activities to a larger forum, then you may want to converse using MU* spaces or IRC. Holding real-time discussions using these environments is one of the most basic, but also most pedagogically valuable, Internet activities; real-time communication will almost certainly transform the interaction that takes place between students.

In a verbal conversation only one person can speak at a time, and usually a handful of outgoing people dominate a discussion. Since every participant in a real-time situation can "talk" at the same time, there is room for much greater involvement. In addition, those students who might have been embarrassed to make an important point face-to-face often feel more comfortable asserting themselves in an electronic message.

Despite the benefits of increased involvement, however, real-time situations can disembody a message from its author, amplifying the tendency of electronic messages to move toward personal rants or flames. The distance that is established between a message and its author can displace the sense of responsibility for language that students should develop. For example, students may inadvertently write a potentially racist, sexist, or homophobic message while participating in real-time discussion. While students often argue that they had not intended to offend, but were "only joking" or "being ironic," they should consider the negative impact of their messages. Instructors can therefore use real-time discussion to explore issues of authorship and responsibility.

Turning these real-time discussions into valuable classroom experiences can be accomplished in part through the use of transcripts. Electronic or printed records of the activities that take place in a MU* can allow for the critical distance needed to analyze the rhetorical situations behind even heated personal interactions. Since brainstorming in real-time is a particularly effective exercise, evaluating transcripts can help solidify some of the free-wheeling exchange that takes place during these sessions.

MU* spaces and IRC lines also free the class from some of the logistical constraints of the traditional classroom. A class that wanted to meet with students from another section or from another institution could log on to a MU* or an IRC environment. Similarly, an instructor could arrange to bring a number of guests from remote locations into the "classroom," or send students into MU*s and IRCs that are frequented by people outside of the class itself. As we have discussed in previous chapters, this kind of interaction with an expanded audience presents an important challenge to writers. They must shape their messages for their readership, and be prepared to receive engaging and sometimes challenging response and feedback.

Constructing Personas

While we've talked about the ways that MU*s and IRCs mediate authorship through electronic messages, we don't want to suggest that they only efface a writer's identity. In fact, one of the values of using IRCs, and probably to a larger extent MU*s, is that they allow students to develop alternative identities. Students can experiment with online constructions of identity and ethos, as well as study audience reaction to various personas. For instance, the appearance of "an elderly, well-dressed African-American woman who would look equally comfortable lecturing in a university or serving food to the homeless with Food Not Bombs" is almost certain to change the flow of a conversation about affirmative action in institutions of higher learning.

MU*s also allow you to control the "gender" of your character in order to move beyond, or at least to examine closely, traditional boundaries of gender and sexuality. Most MU*s give a number of options for gender. Daedalus MOO, for example, lets the user choose from a number of options: either (s/he), egotistical (I), plural (they), royal (we), splat (*e,h*), or even Spivak (e, em, eir, eirs, eirself, E, Em, Eir, Eirs, Eirself). In this way, MU*s and IRCs can liberate participants from the limitations that roles in a physical setting often prescribe for them. This flexibility also provides instructors a means for exploring these roles and stereotypes.

In her article "Gender Swapping on the Internet," Amy Bruckman points out that male students who have played females in MU*s and IRCs often receive an increased amount of attention. For instance, many male characters will "come to the rescue" of female characters, offering assistance which the men logged on as women found condescending. Others have noted a marked increase in sexual advances made toward them when they are logged on as female characters, and many women recommend choosing neutral or male personas in order to avoid harassment. The possibility for these kinds of realizations makes MU*s and IRCs a useful testing ground for understanding the ways that personas can impact and are impacted by the world at large. Even more importantly, most MU*s and IRCs can help interrogate the assumptions which underlie our social interactions.

Despite the suggestion that certain "real-world" benefits can be derived from these environments, some instructors feel that interaction on MU*s and IRCs is frivolous and usually devolves into simple play. We should note, however, that the type of play that occurs in MU*s and IRCs can have a pedagogical value in itself. Play gives us a forum for experimentation—a place to find a voice or test a position—and can compensate for the sometimes debilitating pressures that formal writing assignments put on students. The MU* or IRC environment can release these pressures, and the student who masters words in this environment can bring that sense of mastery to other assignments.

Instructors who plan on using the MU* or IRC environment, then, can work to focus that activity toward helping students with more formal compositions. At the same time, instructors should recognize the interactive experience of MU*s and IRCs as a potentially valuable form of composition. Conversations, for example, often weave together a series of statements with several scripted actions or emotes:

```
Bozo has arrived
You say "Hi Bozo"
Bozo shrugs and throws a sheaf of papers in
the trash
You say "What's that?"
Bozo says "My last English paper"
You say "How did you do"
Bozo grabs his throat in anguish and says
"Forgot to use a title and had three comma-
splices. I choked."
```

One can see that emotes and messages mingle in an environment that is itself sustained by written interactions: speech prompts action and action situates speech, all orchestrated through text.

Constructing Environments

Taken even further, this constructive power of language materializes in the structures that users are able to build in MU*s, in this case by describing them with written text. Indeed, since all activity in MU*s and IRCs is accomplished through written language, students can better understand how our constructions of reality are mediated by language. Students who choose to build structures in a MU*, for example, can experiment with the ways that language constructs realities; written descriptions of virtual structures become particular places, and close attention to language translates into a richer environment.

Building a room in a MU*, for example, requires students to consider the physical details of the surroundings and think about the ways that people will interact in that environment. For instance, a book in a MU* library can be programmed so that a photograph or a page from the author's diary falls from the jacket when a reader picks up the book. A "bot" (short for robot) functioning as a librarian might then be programmed to prompt the reader about connections between the book and the items that were placed in it.

Some Writing-Oriented MU*s That You Might Want to Visit

Diversity University MOO *moo.du.org* 8888
Daedalus MOO *logos.daedalus.com* 7777
Virtual Online University *athena.edu* 8888

In some ways, careful thought about the impact of textual descriptions anticipates many of the activities that might take place in a creative writing class. The well-worn dictum that descriptive writers should "show not tell" is especially pertinent for MU* environments. A room described as "dark and eerie" is less engaging than one depicted as "paneled with mahogany the color of blood." Writing exercises designed to encourage more precise descriptive prose can be easily demonstrated in MU*s and then extended to the explications that students make in all their writing.

Another lesson of MU* construction which can be extended to student work concerns the way that navigation involves a kind of movement through spaces of writing. The details that authors use in their virtual constructions should facilitate this movement, so that a sense of narrative space becomes important. A reader who moves from the library to the bookstore might expect to pass the gas station or the post office, meet someone, see something. What's important is that the writer must consider this movement carefully. Again, we can extend these skills to student writing at large—thinking particularly about the need for clear transitions between ideas and the need for coherence and continuity in an essay.

We should caution that studying these textual constructions requires a good deal of sophistication on the part of students. Additionally, these activities reside on the far end of the MU* and IRC learning curve. We recommend that you consider the range of possibilities provided by MU*s and IRCs—real-time interactions, navigation of pre-existing linguistic spaces, and construction of new linguistic personas and environments—and select the activities which seem the most appropriate for your class. It is important to consider that building on a MU* requires that students have a greater understanding of the technical aspects of MU*s and that instructors have an investment in nontraditional pedagogy. While most of the higher-level MU* activities provide interesting new forums for language use and class activity, they also demand that some priorities be rethought.

HOW CAN YOUR CLASS
USE IRCS AND MU*S? _____

IRC Channels and Online Discussion

Accessing and participating in IRCs is a fairly simple procedure. If you are connected directly to a Unix-based network at your institution, for example, you might simply type "irc" to connect to the IRC server. Often, however, you will use an IRC Client program on your workstation, which provides a much easier interface for your IRC sessions. Some common IRC clients are IRCle (for Macintosh) and MIRC (for Windows). These client programs will have the locations of IRC servers—often more than a hundred—pre-scripted for easy access. You can give students instructions to connect to a specific IRC server, or have them experiment with different servers to see the types of channels that are available on each.

Once you are connected to the IRC, though, you will need to distinguish between commands that you issue to the IRC and the words that you wish to communicate to the group. The first character of a command is always slash (/). Some of the basic commands allow you to list or join channels or modify your nickname. Because the primary purpose of most IRC clients is to facilitate conversation, simply typing a line of text and pressing "enter" will usually send the message to all the users on a currently subscribed IRC channel. Your "nickname" will be attached to the text you write so that the message will automatically be ascribed to you. Thus, after a very brief introduction to the technology, students will find that the operation of IRC discussion is, for the most part, removed to the background.

The different online audiences represented in the channels of the IRC pose an important dilemma for academics interested in using the Internet. Students can interact on existing channels or create a new channel for class discussion. The existing channels provide ways to practice critical reading and to analyze audience (see also our

81

analysis of newsgroups in Chapter Three). Because of the impermanence of the messages and the predominance of channels devoted to virtual sex and tasteless jokes, however, instructors should take care when selecting a channel for class use.

IRC commands

/join #rhetoric
> joins you to an existing channel (here, #rhetoric): if the channel doesn't exist, a new one with that name will be created.

/list
> lists all currently available channels: beware, since there may be thousands of channels available on a single server, listing them all will tie up your machine for several minutes. Type "/help /list" once you are online to manage this list.

/nick newnickname
> changes your nickname to whatever you type in place of "newnickname."

/names
> shows nicknames of users on each channels.

/who channel
> shows who is on a given channel.

/whois nick
> shows "true" identity of someone on a channel.

Unless your goal is to analyze the existing IRC communities with your students, we recommend that you create a new channel for your class. While it is possible that other people may join the channel, an IRC line called, for example, "#rhetoric" will not likely attract someone looking for graphic sexual discussions. To create a new IRC channel, you simply join a channel that doesn't already exist. Choose a name obscure enough that it won't already be in use, but clear enough that it can be recognized. (For a full analysis of the merits of online discussion, see "The Immediacy of Conversation" above.)

Speaking, Emoting, Navigating, and Building

While MU*s offer a greater range of interactivity than the chat channels of IRC, they also require students and instructors to spend more time learning the fundamentals of the medium.

As with e-mail and newsgroups, you can get to a MU* with a simple Telnet connection (see Appendix Four on Telnet) or by using local client software (see Appendix Five on client/server interaction). The simplicity of the connection and the rapidity with which text is transferred on the Internet are two reasons that MU*s have become so popular.

 MU* Clients and Servers

- The most basic login is a Telnet connection directly to the MU*. Enter the IP address followed by the MU* space's port number (usually either 7777 or 8888). For example, the address of Diversity University MOO is *moo.du.org 8888*. The interface provided by this kind of connection, however, is a bit cumbersome. For instance, the new text of other users' messages will scroll onto the screen as you compose new messages, breaking up the text you are trying to enter.

- MU*s can also be accessed by activating a client which resides on a remote machine. Though these programs still rely on a Telnet connection, their interface allows a user to compose more easily and keep a record of the MU* session, although their operation may require knowledge of specialized commands.

- Workstation client applications, available by FTP as freeware, are the easiest way to log on to a MU*. Programs like this assist navigation, offer separate windows for composing messages, and provide easily retrievable transcripts.

(See Appendix Five for more client/server information.)

Many MU*s offer individual accounts to regular visitors with personalized names and passwords, and MU*s have easy-to-use anonymous logins that allow first-time or infrequent users access to the MU*. Check out the best way to get a class online well in advance of visiting, since most MU*s frown on class visits without permission or at least prior notice. Check with MU* administrators for their policies, and make sure that the site you select is reasonable for your class. If you or your students are going to build anything on a MU*, you will probably need to have individual accounts on that server, and permission from its system administrators.

Although some MU*s will require guests to use prefabricated identities, most will allow new users to configure temporary names and descriptions for their characters. By typing the command

```
@desc me as a broad-shouldered guy carrying a
Frisbee
```

a user named "bozo" would set his character description. Any other user who typed

```
look bozo
```

would see "a broad-shouldered guy carrying a Frisbee." Students should take some time to construct a description of themselves as they wish to be seen. The gender of a character is defined by the @gender command; by typing "@gender" followed by "male," "female" or "neuter," you configure the gender of your persona with one of the "traditional" set of gender pronouns. You can usually see the full range of gender options on a MU* by typing "@gender" by itself.

Basic MOO commands

look *x*
> provides a description of the current room unless an object is specified

" *x*
> allows you to "say" whatever you type in after the command

: *x*
> makes your character "emote" whatever you type after the command

whisper "*x*" to *c*
> speaks the message *x* only to the designated character *c*

read *x*
> use to "read" newspapers or signs in MOOs

@desc me as *x*
> provides a description *x* of yourself for those who "look" at you

@gender *x*
> gives your character the gender *x*

@help or **help**
> gives more detailed information about MOO commands and their syntax

(See Appendix Six for more MOO commands.)

The primary interaction that takes place on a MU* is text-based communication. The basic commands are "say" and "emote" (though these can usually be shortened to " and : respectively). The say command (") attributes your name to any message you want to send. For example if your user name is "Athena" and you type in the following line

```
"Nobody knows you're a god on the Internet.
```

everyone in the room (including you) will see the following message appear:

```
Athena says, "Nobody knows you're a god on
the Internet."
```

The say command tells the MU* to place your username and the word "says" in front of exactly what you type.

Similarly, the emote command (:) is used to attribute actions to you. It places your name in front of the text you type after the command. For example, the line

```
:rises in splendor and heads for the nearest
temple.
```

will return the message

```
Athena rises in splendor and heads for the
nearest temple.
```

Though all interaction is thus narrated in third person, it is possible to communicate a wide range of thoughts, emotions, and actions. Since whatever you type after a say or emote command appears on the screen, you can include any number of sentences or any type of ASCII symbol you wish. The most obvious use of this feature is to "say" things with the emote command. By typing a message like

```
:says painfully, "I didn't know that was
going to happen."
```

you will produce

```
Athena says painfully, "I didn't know that
was going to happen."
```

Emoting in third person creates a distance which allows students to express any number of different attitudes toward class discussion, for instance by joking or being ironic. In addition, students must express all communication through their writing rather than rely on tone of voice to express certain subtle feelings.

After having students engage in real-time discussion, and before (or instead of) requiring them to build their own spaces in a MU*, an instructor should consider an intermediary activity—studying existing MU* environments and analyzing the language and rhetorical choices that the authors of the MU* spaces might have made. One of the educationally valuable aspects of MU*s is that in order to navigate, you have to read carefully. The basic navigation commands are simply north, south, east, and west, but rooms in MU*s are built to offer you other possible ranges of motion. A well-constructed room will inform a user about the possible options for movement and investigation. Because this type of interaction on a MU* occurs in writing, it can always be turned into a rhetorical exercise by examining the effectiveness of the writing which shapes a visitor's experience.

Instructors who have access to a MU* might want to build a class site to take full advantage of the possibilities opened by these virtual spaces. You can design interactive sites, present class material, create an online office, construct a room for class discussions, or add a wing for students to build spaces and class projects (see Appendix Six for a brief list of building commands).

Since most instructors are not likely to spend the time it takes to have their students build projects on a MU*, we have geared this chapter primarily toward real-time communication and interaction. However, if you are interested in putting student projects on a MU*, see our Case Study below. We also suggest that you keep these strategies in mind:

- limit the scope of MU* projects;
- keep the projects focused on rhetorical concerns;
- allow extra time to learn MU* skills;
- build in a process of revision; and
- consider using collaborative groups.

Keep in mind also that the composition that takes place in MU* building is descriptive. Thus, building spaces on a MU* can enhance creative writing skills, but making a major project more useful for a general composition course requires a substantial commitment to this new form. The high percentage of descriptive rather than analytical text needed to construct a MU* environment shifts the focus away from argumentation. Meanwhile, the technical training necessary to produce sophisticated, interactive spaces on a MU* can hamper the quality and variety of projects.

Introductory Exercises: IRCs and MU*s

- Have students seek out an IRC channel of personal interest and participate on their own time, to practice basic skills such as using nicknames, and distinguishing between messages sent to the discussion participants, and commands issued to the IRC. • Use real-time discussion in the IRCs (or a virtual environment in a MU* which has been developed for course goals) to enable students to role-play different characters or perspectives, and develop positions for written assignments. • Provide students with a list of MU* addresses and an assignment to visit several, in order to get a feel for their features and organizational possibilities.

Sample Assignments

- Conduct an IRC/MU* session where students and the instructor log on from remote sites to simulate distance learning possibilities. It's possible to have the instructor or "connected" students log on from home, or have visitors log on from another site anywhere in the world. Stress the type of interaction that is possible, including its limitations. (This exercise can be compared to a similar e-mail assignment examined in the Chapter Two Case Study.)

- Have your class visit several MU* spaces and evaluate their experiences with the text-based environment (for a list of possible spaces to visit, see the sample MU*s above). This assignment can range from discussing initial impressions of a MU*, to a much more specific analysis of the ways a particular room or site constructs an experience for the visitor, including critiques of how the writing might be made stronger.

- Develop a simple MU* environment to see what the role-playing capabilities of MU*s can add to a debate (for example, by reenacting and analyzing a rhetorical problem presented in a book, film or other cultural text). In order to give students a deeper understanding of characters' motivations, ask them to role-play individuals from the text.

- Have your class build a set of rooms relating to a course topic. Try to incorporate strategies of argument into the environment's descriptions.

*Chapter Four: IRCs and MU*s*

MU* CASE STUDY

E309K From Scribe to Cyborg: Technology's
Effect on Self-Expression
Instructor: Jean Lee Cole

This case study examines a pair of student-built MU* projects designed for a writing course that investigated the sociological impact
of technology on textual production. The title of the course, "From
Scribe to Cyborg: Technology's Effect on Self-Expression," describes
well its theme and historical scope.

Students were instructed to research "the effect of at least two different technologies we've discussed this semester on one socio-political
aspect of culture: for example, business, education, advertising, art,
gender relations, revolutionary politics, etc.," and present that research in one of four media. The description of the MU* option
read as follows:

> AcademICK, the English Department's very own
> text-based virtual reality space, is cur-
> rently under construction. For this
> project, you and several others will be
> designing a small "virtual exhibit" that
> will teach future visitors about the effect
> of communications technology on society.
> You may want to present information in the
> form of a virtual slide show, a "skit"
> peopled by some of the writers we've dis-
> cussed, or a "hands-on" demonstration.
> Groups of 2 or 3 are ideal for this project;
> outside help with programming and other
> technical issues will be available.

(Note that AcademICK, the virtual environment discussed here,
actually uses TinyMUSH programming language. However, in keep-

ing with our terminology throughout this chapter, we will continue
to refer to this assignment as a MU* project.)

This instructor included MU*s in her syllabus only to the extent
that she felt was merited by her particular course. She says the
experience of building a MU* is much more pedagogically useful
than "running around in one," and she was not particularly interested in using pre-existing MU*s themselves as material for rhetorical analysis (which is one pedagogical strategy we discuss above).
Yet, she did not want to invest in the MU*s to the extent of making
them a major component of the course. Giving students the choice
of whether or not to work with MU*s struck an important balance
for her, ensuring that only students interested in the concept would
have to invest the time to learn the basics, but that simultaneously,
the ones who did engage the MU* medium did so much more actively.

Rhetorically, the text-based nature of MU*s makes them an interesting alternative to traditional writing assignments, since this project
focuses students' attention on writing, particularly in descriptions of
the environment and in the need to present research findings to the
user in novel ways. Since MU*s work more like fiction than linear
argumentation, students working in these environments have to weave
argument implicitly into descriptions of the MU* space and the objects it contains, rather than present an explicit thesis.

The first group project featured in this case study focuses on a print
shop from the era of handset type, and a corporate office space. The
rhetorical purpose of their project is to examine the influence of
communications technology on gender stereotypes in the workplace.
The first environment in their exhibit makes use of an automated
guide in the person of Mark Twain, and gives the user the opportunity to examine the components of the shop—presses, type cases and
other tools—and to have conversations with the shop employees,
such as the compositor and pressman. The purpose of this particular
environment is to demonstrate the way such a workplace has histori-

cally been constructed as a male space. All of the shop's employees
are noticeably male; for example, the pressman is described as follows:

> This burly guy looks like someone you would
> NOT want to be up against on American Gladi-
> ators. His right arm looks much stronger
> than his left from pulling the lever on the
> press. His clothes are worn and stained with
> ink and sweat.

A fair amount of research on the part of students went into this
project, visible especially in the historically accurate descriptions of
early printing press technology:

> Two vertical columns of wood bolted to the
> floor and stabilized by wooden girders at-
> tached to the ceiling. Between them is a
> large plate, called the platen, mounted on a
> wide screw that is operated by a large le-
> ver. Two rails extend from underneath the
> platen so the press bed can be loaded with
> the imposed formes (the completed pages of
> type). A pad, called the tympan, is attached
> to the press bed by hinges. The blank sheet
> of paper is placed here for printing.

as well as in the commentary offered by Twain, the guide:

> Mark Twain says "Before the printing-press,
> the job of copying books was left to
> scribes. These were monks who devoted their
> lives to this art. They had all the respon-
> sibility of the entire job. The printing
> press allowed the task to be split into
> several more specialized tasks, and thus
> created the different jobs performed by each
> of the men you see here."

93

Additionally, the students designed the environment so that by interacting with Twain, the user is able to initiate a demonstration of the printing process using this early technology.

The second environment in the first group's exhibit is the office of the Remington Rand Corporation, in which a historical context for the invention and marketing of the typewriter is presented. The "steno pool" of Remington Rand is constructed as a stereotypically female space. Hints about the historical development of this stereotype are strategically placed throughout the environment. For example, when the user examines one of the typewriters, the following description is offered:

```
A shiny black (manual) typewriter is being
used by Miss Lilly. (Electrics aren't around
yet) Remington Rand Inc. began by making
guns, then diversified to sewing-machines
that they decorated with flowery gold de-
signs for the ladies. When they further
diversified into typewriters, they saw them
as something women would use. That is why
this one is so ornate.
```

The principle behind this environment is that the user is there for a job interview. In the office environment, as well the print shop, the group makes excellent use of MU* characteristics to create an interesting rhetorical situation. In the office, users whose gender is defined as female are interviewed for secretarial positions, while "males" are interviewed for management positions. Analogous gender differences are built into the print shop environment as well. Of course, the students built such stereotypes into their project not to perpetuate them, but in an attempt to create an experience which would lead the user to contemplate these stereotypes and their relationship to the development of communications technology.

The second group planned a much more expansive project, working with the metaphor of an amusement park to present a great deal of information to the user. In discussions with this group, the instructor repeatedly encouraged its members to limit their scope—advice which they did not heed. The group intended to explore the idea of life with computers and "post-computers," looking at technology's effects upon literary genres (more specifically, different styles of science fiction). Although this second group contained more experienced MU* users than the first group, the final results of this project were somewhat confusing. Because of their greater familiarity with MU* commands and the capabilities of the medium, a lot of flashy elements were built in (such as an object which would "teleport" the user to another location). However, the rhetorical purpose of the overall project is not clear, and it does not come as close to meeting the requirements of the assignment as does the first group's project.

Rather than working closely together, the group—again perhaps because each of them felt comfortable working alone in the medium—divided the project up, each student working on a separate "room" in the environment. As a result of this division, and the lack of communication between students, the instructor feels the connections between different elements of the project are somewhat flimsy. The only connection, in fact, is the metaphor of a ride in the amusement park—the user moves from room to room on a sort of trolley.

Nevertheless, some elements of the project are successful. For example, the group demonstrates extensive research about an older computer technology:

```
To the left, you see a desk-sized control
console which has one large panel of lights,
buttons, and dials. Next to it is a small
rolling table which has a typewriter-style
interface. To the right is a bank of mag-
netic tape units. To the back is a large
gray metal housing, about fourteen feet
long, seven feet wide, and nine feet tall.
```

> There are five doors with silver handles in
> the housing. Three pipes lead from the top
> of the housing into the ceiling, one at the
> end and two in the middle. A strip of chrome
> near the top of the housing has raised let-
> ters spelling UNIVAC. The loud whirring and
> humming of the machine never ceases.

The research going into these descriptions, however, does not produce an environment whose rhetorical purpose is readily ascertainable.
At certain points, the experience is almost bewildering:

> You see a green ziggurat reaching high above
> the street. Its walls sparkle with the en-
> trances and exits of personal icons. One
> personal icon in particular seems to be
> heading for the ziggurat at high speed. The
> area of the building which meets the icon's
> trajectory begins to glow bright chartreuse.
> Just before the icon reaches the wall, a
> bolt of green light shoots out and hits the
> icon, which promptly disappears from the
> Matrix. As should be obvious from the IC,
> this is _not_ a public building.

The students who created the second project are obviously quite
innovative and should, perhaps under different circumstances, be
encouraged to pursue their interests in MU*s as a creative outlet.
The amusement park project, however, does little to demonstrate
their understanding of the societal effects of technology (which was
the rhetorical purpose of the assignment).

Ultimately, the instructor feels, the second project attempts much
more than it actually accomplishes. Because MU* building involves
learning a mode of discourse different from ones with which we are
familiar, students should heed the advice that beginning with a somewhat limited scope can help ensure that the spaces they build are

more fully developed and work towards meeting the goals of the assignment.

In retrospect, perhaps because of the project produced by the second group, the instructor feels that the MU* technology may have distracted her students from the assignment's rhetorical goals. She suggests that, if she were to use MU*s again, she might offer a much more focused assignment—for example, asking students to design a room which is intended to evoke a specific kind of experience for the user. With a less expansive assignment, students might focus more clearly on the rhetorical consequences of their design choices.

There are many disincentives to the use of MU*s for which instructors must compensate: the occasional tendency of real-time discussion to drift toward immaturity, the steep learning curve for MU* building, the possibility of students focusing too much on what can be achieved in terms of MU* navigation while neglecting the rhetorical purpose of their projects. However, the first example from this case study demonstrates that when the characteristics of MU*s mesh with the purposes of the course, this medium can produce insightful student projects.

97

Chapter Four: IRCs and MU*s

Chapter Five
The Electronic Library: Browsing with Gopher and the World Wide Web

5

WHAT IS BROWSING THE NET?_____

As the term "information superhighway" suggests, one of the most highly touted aspects of the Internet has been its tremendous potential as a research tool. However, in order to incorporate the seemingly limitless resources that are available online into a classroom situation successfully, students need to learn effective Internet research strategies. Though we call this process of researching with the Internet "browsing," the term encompasses more than the traditional notion of walking through a section of the library and choosing books off the shelf. While browsing the Internet, a user connects to different sites around the world, actively explores directories of information, performs automated keyword searches of multiple files, and downloads and saves any useful resources, including graphic, sound and video files.

Key Terms

Bookmark: an electronic pointer to a Gopher, FTP or Web site that can be recalled for future reference. A list of bookmarks is known as a "hotlist."

Downloading: retrieving a file or application from a remote host over the Internet.

FTP (File Transfer Protocol): an early system of downloading and uploading files across the Internet. Although somewhat basic, FTP is still frequently used.

Gopher: a system of Internet protocols and directory structures that allows users to connect to remote hosts, to access directories of information, and to download files. In addition, Gopher sites can be searched for directory names, file titles, or text contained in individual files.

Gopher Client: a program which provides an easy interface for searching and accessing documents and directories in Gopherspace.

Gopher Server: also referred to as a "Gopherhost." A centralized server that offers hierarchically organized information to a user via a Gopher client.

Search Engine: a device that performs keyword searches on the Internet (e.g., Veronica, WAIS, WebCrawler).

Surfing: the process of navigating from site to site on the Internet (usually the Web) in a non-linear and non-hierarchical manner.

Targeting: connecting directly to a Gopherhost or Web site by entering a known address.

Tunneling: accessing a site (usually a Gopher site) by digging down through various directories or sub-directories.

URL (Uniform Resource Locator): the address assigned to each file on the World Wide Web.

Web Browser: client software used for navigating and interacting with the World Wide Web. The Web browser translates the HTML source documents that reside on the Web into a fluid, multimedia interface.

Web Server: a server equipped with software to facilitate the Hypertext Transfer Protocol (HTTP) that enables documents to be linked and shared on the Web. Users can access the documents stored on Web servers with a Web browser.

World Wide Web: abbreviated *WWW* or *the Web*. Distributed hypermedia system built upon older protocols (FTP, Gopher, etc.) and additional newer protocols (HTTP). WWW client software provides the ability to view many types of files (HTML, GIF, text, etc.).

Gopher

Browsing on the Internet was first made possible by Gopher, a set of protocols which allowed users to access different machines worldwide and to view directory structures and available files. Along with a new ability to be moved fluidly from one site to another, Gopher provided a more user-friendly interface for file transfer protocol (FTP), the system which allows files to move from one site to another (see Appendix Four for FTP information). Through Gopher, a user could for the first time easily browse the contents of Internet hosts and retrieve the files stored there. Computer science departments, libraries, and later academic institutions, quickly adopted this medium as a way to disseminate and share information.

Although Gopher functions have changed somewhat (now often performed by Web browsing applications), there are still three primary strategies for finding specific information using Gopher:

- Students can "target" a specific machine (a Gopherhost) whose address they know, and hunt through the site.

- Students can access a number of Gopherhosts and "tunnel" through them, exploring geographically organized directories as well as subject trees containing directories like "Libraries," "Government," and "Jobs." Since they are organized hierarchically, Gopher sites can structure the wealth of information on the Internet in helpful ways. A user can move up or down through a Gopher site with some sense of direction. For instance, a user who was looking for information at MIT could follow the path "World/North America/United States/Massachusetts/MIT."

- Students can perform keyword searches of Gopherspace in order to retrieve files or directories containing those keywords.

The materials uncovered when browsing a Gopher site can vary significantly from those found on other Internet media. Gopher sites are maintained by individual institutions and updated as new material is created, formatted, and approved. As a result, files on the sites can be extremely current (for instance, newsgroup and e-mail postings) or authoritative (archival research material). Gopher sites can store some of the most recent and extensive research in a field, online library catalogs, an institution's academic calendar and a variety of other materials.

The World Wide Web

Browsing the World Wide Web, like searching with Gopher, allows users to access and download files at a site, examine and explore broad topic categories, and perform a multitude of keyword search functions. However, unlike Gopher, where a user will tunnel up or down among hierarchies, the hypertextual capabilities of the Web allow connections between documents regardless of their location.

A single Web page can display multimedia files and link to other documents on local or remote servers. A page might link to a sound file at an FTP site in Australia, a text file from a Gopher site in Europe and a graphic file from a Web server in Idaho. In addition, most Web browsers now incorporate Internet technologies, like Gopher and newsgroups, which previously demanded their own client applications. The allure of the connectivity and multimedia possibilities of the Web have in great part led to the recent growth of the Internet.

We will discuss the hypertextual possibilities of composing with the Web in our next chapter, but for now, we will try to equip you with the best ways to implement Internet browsing in your classroom. The remainder of this chapter will discuss in more detail the value of browsing for student research. It will also offer some helpful advice on browsing strategies and conclude with a sample browsing session illustrating the narrowing of a research topic and the gathering of Internet resources. For information about documenting the sources that you find, we discuss citation issues in Appendix Three.

 Search Clients and Servers

- Gopher and Web clients can reside on remote computers and can be accessed with a simple Telnet connection. With Gopher, these clients are fairly effective. A user will generally select items from a menu by entering the number that corresponds to the function they wish to perform. Because Web pages contain multimedia elements, however, these Telnet connections severely limit text-only Web browsers.

- Along with an easier interface, Gopher clients which reside on individual workstations offer several other advantages. A user can create bookmarks, save text files, download and open graphic or sound files and record a navigational history.

- Of all the client software we discuss in this book, workstation Web browsers are the most essential for taking full advantage of the capabilities of the Internet. Web browsers have subsumed some of the functions of e-mail, newsgroups, Gopher, Telnet, and FTP. In addition, these clients "seamlessly" weave together the multimedia resources of the Web. Besides offering navigational aids like bookmarks or hotlists, Web browsing clients offer a number of other features, some of which will be discussed in Chapter Six.

(See Appendix Five for more client/server information.)

WHY BROWSE THE NET? —————

Research, Discovery, and Analysis

Instructors who seriously wish to incorporate online resources into their pedagogy will benefit from educating themselves and their students about productive strategies for browsing. Although browsing may offer few opportunities for writing, it is a crucial research skill that instructors will want to teach to their students. Browsing the net will provide students with excellent material for their papers and projects. More importantly, it can help teach them about the necessity of narrowing their topics, evaluating source material and effectively incorporating online research into their writing.

Browsing in Gopherspace or on the Web (more likely the latter), researchers will encounter: copies of traditional print journals, electronic journals, online reference materials like encyclopedias, archives of newsgroup or listserv postings, institutional publications (academic, corporate, nonprofit, etc.), personal commentary, and the various forms of conversation found on the Internet. In certain areas— "third world" news, computer related information, environmental issues, political discussion, and many others—the net offers unparalleled resources. Similarly, as a storehouse for official documents of all types, and for information about extremely current events, Gopher and Web sites contain a wealth of material that can easily be utilized by instructors and students.

While there is an incredible volume and range of resource material available online, researching with the Internet presents students with certain difficulties. First, online information exists on different servers all over the world, and although this information may be organized locally, nowhere is there a comprehensive list of available resources. Second, material on the Internet is often ephemeral. As servers are reorganized, site addresses changed, and documents replaced, information that is available one day can be gone the next. Finally, because of the tremendous growth of the Internet, and especially of the Web, new information is being added hourly. Searches will often produce different results as new documents come online, complicating the notion of a comprehensively researched topic.

Although these and other difficulties exist for online researchers, the fundamental techniques involved in using the Internet as a research tool are quite similar to library research skills. Topics still have to be narrowed, searches refined, and source materials evaluated. For classes that have easy access to Gopher and Web browsers, the Internet offers a very effective place for students to begin gathering material for research projects and to develop research skills.

Browsing can be incorporated effectively into any stage of a student's research. For students who have not yet decided on a paper topic, tunneling through Gopherspace, surfing the Web, or performing key-word searches can serve as initial brainstorming techniques. Once a broad topic has been settled upon, running a more extensive set of keyword searches can help narrow and refine the topic (see the Case Study below for an extended example of this process). Finally, browsing can help students investigate the availability of material in order to assess the scholarship on a given topic. These stages mirror the process of developing a good thesis and a strong argument in student research projects.

Browsing also provides instructors with another arena in which to discuss the importance of evaluating source material. As is the case when using most Internet research tools, browsing Gopherspace and the Web will generally turn up a wide range of information—both in terms of quantity and quality. A student researching human rights abuses in East Timor, for example, will likely need to balance the various authorities of material published by government organiza-tions like the CIA, non-governmental organizations (NGOs) like Amnesty International, corporate organizations like CitiBank who wish to invest in the region, academic observers like Noam Chomsky, and a host of individuals who may have collected information and "published" their opinions about the situation. With this range of authors, students could very likely find themselves in the uncomfort-able position of needing to compare a well-written, well-researched article taken from a Gopher site (and therefore displayed in unformatted, ASCII text), with information that may be less rel-evant, but which is part of a well-designed Web site complete with stylish text layout, graphics, video, and sound. As we discuss in Chapters Two and Three, instructors should survey this range of information, authority, and rhetorical persuasiveness with their stu-dents in order to address the potential advantages and disadvantages of using nontraditional source material in research projects.

HOW CAN YOUR CLASS
BROWSE THE NET?⎯⎯⎯⎯⎯⎯⎯⎯

As we suggested earlier in this chapter, our concept of "browsing" includes both Gopher and the World Wide Web. As we also mentioned earlier in this chapter, strategies for browsing (whether through Gopher or the Web) fall into three broad categories: connecting directly to a known site (which we call "targeting"), following paths and links to search for materials ("tunneling" or "surfing"), and making use of keyword searches.

Targeting a Specific Site

While the software you use to browse Gopherspace will probably be configured to use your institution's host, you will be able to begin another Gopher session by entering an alternate Gopher address. Gopherhost addresses are machine names; therefore, they look much like the portion of an e-mail address following the "@" symbol. For instance, one might connect directly to the host *Gopher2.tc.umn.edu* at the University of Minnesota, the institution where Gopher was first developed.

If you already know the location of a site, you can search it out by moving through a sequence of geographical hierarchies. Although this process involves the techniques of tunneling, we include it in the discussion of targeting because the user is trying to reach a specific destination. For those who cannot enter a Gopherhost address directly, this method of targeting will be the easiest way to locate a particular Gopher site. For example, say that you wanted to connect to the Gopher archive called the Latin America Network Information Center (sponsored by the Institute for Latin American Studies at the University of Texas). You would most likely select a directory called "World," after which you would move through a series of progressively narrower hierarchies. From the "World" directory you would first choose "North America," then "United States," then "Texas," then "University of Texas at Austin." You would then choose "Colleges and Departments," then "College of Liberal Arts," then "LANIC." Note also that once you have located a useful site, using the bookmark feature of your client software can allow you to jump directly to that spot without having to follow the full path again.

When using the Web, the strategy of targeting becomes much more important for the simple reason that each file has its own specific address (URL). Since the Web is not organized in clear hierarchical directories, following paths to specific sites or documents can be quite difficult. For this reason targeting is the primary means of locating information; at any point a user can enter a URL and connect directly to a desired page or file. Since locating a site often depends upon knowing its address, URLs are frequently distributed on e-mail listservs and newsgroups in order to publicize the sites to interested audiences.

Tunneling Gophers and Web Surfers

Subject directories (or "trees") are a good starting point for students who have a broad idea of their topic but do not yet have a keyword narrow enough to bring back a manageable amount of material (see "Keyword Searches" below). The trick for you and your students is finding a good set of subject trees. If you are at an institution that provides its own Gopherhost, check there first to see what subject categories are available to you. If not, you might try initiating your research from a well-established site like the University of Minnesota. Since seeking out a good subject tree on another Gopher host can be rather difficult, and since subject trees in Gopher are generally not very well developed, we also suggest exploring a World Wide Web resource, such as Yahoo or Infoseek, which abound with complex subject trees that can lead you to useful topic-specific resources.

Ironically, although the Web provides far more useful subject directories, the idea of hierarchical structure is somewhat antithetical to the Web, where the vertical model of "tunneling" is often replaced by the less structured metaphor of "surfing." While the designers of many Web search engines have utilized subject trees, the Web itself is not hierarchical, as is the directory and file structure of Gopher. The hypertextual capabilities of the Web allow creators of home pages to provide links to related material, which in turn have links to further material. Advise your students that because the paths they take while surfing the Web may be difficult to replicate, they should make use of bookmarks to note the location of sites they find useful.

Keyword Searches

Boolean Operators

Most of the engines for keyword searches use some form of Boolean operators to modify search strings. Employing these commands allows the user to narrow a search and to bring back a smaller number of "hits." We list some of the basic commands here, with which you may be familiar from searching various library databases (such as the MLA online index). If your class is going to make use of Internet browsing, we recommend you discuss Boolean operators with your students early in the semester, and stress that the same basic techniques will be useful in a number of different Internet environments.

Entering	Searches for
term1 term2 term3	all occurrences of either term1 or term2 or term3
term1 AND term2	only occurrences of both terms 1 and 2
term1 OR term2	either term1 or term2
term1 NOT term2	only occurrences of term1 which do not contain term2
term1*	occurrences of the root within other words (a "Fuzzy Search" of term1)

"term1 term2 term3"   only occurrences of all three terms together
(a "Literal Search")

The terms can also be used in conjunction with one another. For example the search pattern

racial OR sexual AND discrimination OR bias

would produce a series of hits containing any combination of the following phrases: racial discrimination, sexual discrimination, racial bias, sexual bias (but not occurrences of only one of the terms on its own).

Not every search engine uses Boolean operators in exactly the same way. Check the information provided at the site of the search engine to find out which functions are supported.

WAIS

WAIS, the Wide Area Information Search, is a tool that helps users locate and extract information from a collection of documents. It is a long-standing public domain search engine, whose name is now something of a misnomer. The search covers a "wide area" in that it allows you to search multiple databases, but its area of coverage is narrower than more recently-developed tools which search multiple hosts worldwide. WAIS searches only a limited number of databases, and requires that certain connections be established between the WAIS software and the text to be searched. WAIS searches are employed on Gopher sites, on Web sites, and on local databases.

Although (or perhaps because) WAIS covers a narrower body of materials than other searches, some of its search capabilities are more powerful. Many WAIS hosts will allow you to search the complete text of documents for your keywords, instead of just their titles or subject lines (as Veronica does, for example). Most WAIS applications support Boolean search strings, which will constitute the primary method for you or your students to narrow your searches. For more information about the capabilities of WAIS and the material it covers at a particular site, look for a "readme" or FAQ file located on the site.

Veronica

Veronica is an index and retrieval system which can locate items on 99% of the Gopher servers around the world. As of January 1995 (the most recent figures available), the Veronica index contained about fifteen million items from approximately 15,000 servers.

To initiate a Veronica search, you must first connect to a site (located in cities like New York, Pisa, Koeln, and Bergen) which offers the service. Once you log on to a Veronica host, you will be asked to enter a search string. Note that Veronica searches for words in titles of resources; it does not do a full-text search of the contents of the resources.

If a Veronica search returns few or no resources, you can broaden the search without changing keywords. Veronica makes use of the asterisk wildcard; using it tells the computer to search for all occurrences of the root within other words (but the asterisk can only be used at the end of the root, not at the beginning or in the middle). This can be especially helpful, since the titles of Gopher files are often abbreviated to save space. A search for
```
envir*
```
will not only turn up titles for environment, environmental, environmentalism, etc., but also a file named "environ.amazon.txt."

A Veronica search will produce a list of items very similar to WAIS results. The primary difference is that the items contained in it point to sites all over the world rather than on the same host. Research can thus be compounded by certain problems. With the duplication of materials on the Internet, different listings might actually take the user to the same resource, stored on two or more different sites. Additionally, certain sites may temporarily be down, or too busy to allow connections. For these reasons, you should save the search results as a file so that you can return to those sites when the connections are re-established.

Web Research Sites

One of the features that makes the Web so powerful is its ability to accommodate the protocols of earlier Internet media, thus subsuming the once separate features of newsgroups, Gopher, FTP, Telnet and other Internet media. All of the materials located on Gopherhosts can also be accessed through a Web browser, and the keyword searches described above can all be replicated on the Web. Additionally, the Web provides numerous keyword search engines of its own. An important characteristic of Web search tools is that they often allow not only a variety of different keyword searches but also some form of subject directories. While some guides to the Internet make a sharp distinction between Web search engines which provide directories organized by subject and those which provide keyword searches, in reality this is something of a false distinction. More and more common are the Web research tools which integrate both of these elements into a single, fluid interface.

The best way to begin a keyword search (indeed, any kind of search) on the Web is to find a "jump station," a Web page with links to various search engines, and, ideally, brief descriptions of each. If your institution does not support such a page, and you are not already familiar with one, we recommend you try the list at the University of Texas at Austin (*http://www.utexas.edu/search/*). Netscape's Net Search Directory is also an excellent location to begin a Web search. Connect to *http://home.netscape.com/escapes/search/* or, if you are using a Netscape Web browser, simply click on the "Net Search" button on the toolbar. In general, subject directories provide a good overview of the Internet material available on broadly defined topics, and are therefore a good tool for the early stages of a research project. Keyword searches enable much more comprehensive re-search on a topic, and are most useful when a student has identified several keywords which will help him narrow the focus of his re-search. Browsing subject directories can help identify sub-categories of the broader topic, providing these additional keywords.

The Web search tools described below represent only some of the innumerable research sites and search engines available on the Web (in contrast to Gopher, where only a handful exist). Whichever search you choose, the results will be returned to you as a list of hypertext links. Note that because some of the search engines scan the full text of files rather than just their titles, the items listed will not necessarily contain your keyword. You will sometimes need to follow even seemingly unrelated links to evaluate their usefulness. The list of search returns can be saved as a file and accessed during later sessions; however, to preserve the items as active links (and not just text), you must save the files in HTML format.

All-in-One Search Page
http://www.albany.net/allinone/

A useful resource to search for information with a wide variety of sources all from one site. The All-in-One Search Page, with more than 200 search tools in all, works by compiling search forms for all Web search engines. Search easily in categories such as: World Wide Web, General Interest, People, News, Publications, Desk Reference. (Note: the "categories" do not function like subject-directory trees for browsing, but are rather compilations of keyword search engines.) Once you perform a search, you will be connected to that particular search engine's home page, and can utilize all its features; to return to the All-in-One Search Page, use the "back" arrow or the list of recent URLs on your Web browser's menu bar (on Netscape, this is the "Go" menu).

Alta Vista
  http://altavista.digital.com/

A project sponsored by the Digital Equipment Corporation, Alta Vista provides a very fast search of either the Web or Usenet newsgroups. Alta Vista's real strength is its keyword search, which encompasses more than 30 million Web pages and several million newsgroup messages. Alta Vista will generally return more extensive results than other search tools, but more evaluation is required of the researcher to sift through this material to find the most relevant items. The advanced features of the Alta Vista search allow you to control both the selection criteria (Boolean terms, including NEAR), as well as "results ranking criteria" (matching documents are ranked according to a grade based on how many of the search terms each document contains, where the words are in the document, and how close to each other they are). While Alta Vista does not offer subject directories, it does offer a "random jumps" feature which is designed "to allow you to visit places in the Web you would never suspect existed." By choosing one of fifteen different general categories (e.g. Art, Interviews, Universities), a user is connected to a randomly-selected Web page. While the "random jumps" feature is a novel way of exploring the Web, it is not an especially useful tool for topic-driven academic research.

The Argus Clearinghouse
  http://www.clearinghouse.net/

A central access point for guides which identify, describe, and evaluate Internet-based resources. Designed by librarians from the University of Michigan who share the belief that "intellectual labor is necessary to provide a qualitative assessment of the Internet's information," the Clearinghouse is primarily for a specialized research and university audience. Guides on specific topics can be retrieved either with a keyword search, or by browsing through the subject directories, beginning with these primary categories: Arts and Humanities, Business and Employment, Communication, Computers and

Information Technology, Education, Engineering, Environment, Government and Law, Health and Medicine, Places and Peoples, Recreation, Science and Mathematics, Social Sciences, and Social Issues. An additional component of the Argus Clearinghouse is the "Internet Searching Center," which provides a simple index to the Internet tools and resources the Argus staff find to be the most useful.

ElNet Galaxy
http://www.einet.net/

The ElNet Galaxy includes both a keyword search engine and subject directories. The keyword search supports Boolean operators and provides the option of searching the Galaxy pages (the subject trees and other pages on the Galaxy site), menu titles in Gopherspace, "hytelnet" (a hypertext database of Telnet sites), or the entire World Wide Web (complete text of documents, or the title or link texts only). The subject trees are intended for a professional audience in each category: Business and Commerce, Engineering and Technology, Government, Humanities, Law, Medicine, Reference, Science, Social Science. They provide general information that may interest the student researcher, but also professional information (announcements, links to professional organizations) that most likely will not.

Excite
http://www.excite.com/

Excite Search offers a feature its creators proudly call searching the Web "by concept." That is, Excite's keyword feature not only searches for combinations of the search terms you enter, but also conceptually related terms. The search engine is programmed to recognize a connection between terms like, for example, "elderly people" and "senior citizens." If a researcher enters "elderly people," Excite also searches automatically for documents containing the term "senior citizens." The scope of a keyword search can be set for the entire World Wide Web, an "Excite Web Guide" of 150,000 pages carefully selected "by Excite's experts," Usenet newsgroups, or "NewsTracker" (articles from over 300 Web-based publications). In addition to standard Boolean operators, Excite offers features which the user should read about before performing an advanced search: for example, a "more like this" link, radio buttons, and plus and minus signs. Excite's subject indices organize by the following broad categories: Arts and Entertainment, Business and Investing, Careers and Education, Computers and Internet, Games, Health and Science, Lifestyles, My Channel (a personalized information page with complex features), News, People and Chat, Politics, Shopping, Sports, Travel, and Regional.

Infoseek
http://www.infoseek.com/

A good index of Web resources, for a general audience. Infoseek claims to have the world's largest directory of categorized Web pages (eclipsing Yahoo! in June, 1996). The directory is divided into these primary categories: Arts and Entertainment, Business, Computers, Education, Finance and Investment, Getting It Done (employment and finance issues), Health, Internet, Kids and Family Fun, Politics, Shopping, Sports, Travel, and Leisure. Infoseek offers a "desk reference" section including Webster's dictionary, Roget's thesaurus and Bartlett's Quotations, as well as extensive directories of e-mail addresses, yellow pages, city maps, area codes, and zip codes.

Infoseek provides two distinct keyword search tools: Ultrasmart, with "comprehensive query results," and Ultraseek, a streamlined tool for "power users who know what they want and want it fast." To enable users to narrow search results quickly, each new Ultrasmart query searches within your previous results (unless you specify otherwise). A drop-down menu allows researchers to search other sets of information besides Web pages: Usenet newsgroups, news wire services, "premiere news" (from seven major national news organizations), e-mail addresses, company profiles, and Web FAQs. Many reviews of Infoseek praise the timeliness of its information, and its visually appealing interface compared to other search tools.

Inter-Links
http://alabanza.com/kabacoff/Inter-Links/

The Inter-Links home page offers a broad variety of features: links to all the major Internet search tools through the heading "Search the Net," links to online books and magazines and to "thousands of libraries," a Reference Shelf of dictionaries, encyclopedias and other sources of information, as well as categories for "News and Weather" and an extensive set of Internet and Web guides and tutorials. Inter-Links also offers Web subject directories under the heading "topical resources," the primary divisions being: Diversity, Education, Employment, Fine Arts, Government, Health and Medicine, Law, Math and Science, and Psychology.

The Internet Public Library
http://www.ipl.org/

The organization of this resource recalls that of a more traditional public library, with departments such as Reference, Teen, Youth, Magazines and Serials, and Exhibits. Reference works and search tools include not only those categorized by the IPL, but some created by them as well (for example, a guide to the best search engines on the Web, with tips on how to use them effectively). Online serial publications can be searched by keyword or browsed by title, in alphabetical order or by subject. Permanent Exhibits in the IPL's "Exhibition Hall" include photographic essays and other works, on topics of American history and cultures. Hundreds of newspapers from dozens of countries are online and searchable at the IPL. Mimicking a reference desk where a researcher has the opportunity to ask questions of a librarian, the IPL offers interactive forms to allow you to send detailed questions to their reference staff.

The Internet Services List
http://www.spectracom.com/islist/

A resource with a simple hierarchy good for researchers new to the Web. The site offers a subject-directory listing of around eighty categories, from Agriculture to the World Wide Web. The Internet Services List does not itself offer a keyword search, but links to many search tools which do, either in local databases or "globally." The Internet Services List links to many Web sites, but also Gopher, Telnet and FTP resources that might not be uncovered by other search tools.

Library of Congress World Wide Web Home Page
http://lcWeb.loc.gov/

First and foremost, this site is an Internet showcase for the U.S. Library of Congress, and reflects all the resources of its analogue in the physical world. The "American Memory" section presents extensive resources in American history. The THOMAS database provides full-text access to current bills under consideration in the U.S. Congress, and other Legislative resources; additional databases cover the other branches of the federal government, as well as state and local governments. Exhibitions in the Library of Congress are preserved in an online format on the site. Extensive Internet access is provided to the resources of the Library of Congress (e.g. the catalog, the research department). The entire Web site of the Library of Congress can be searched by keyword. The home page also organizes Internet resources into an extensive set of subject-categories, and links to multiple keyword search engines (for the Web as well as Gopher, FTP and Telnet sites).

Lycos
http://lycos.cs.cmu.edu/

The All-in-One page states that the "new" Lycos now indexes more than 90% of the Web. Reliable and fast, Lycos allows custom searching. It uses the matching parameters "loose," "fair" "good," "close," and "strong," but doesn't explain precisely how they narrow the search (although they clearly do). Users can also specify how many of their terms the search engine should match at one time. Lycos indexes FTP and Gopher sites, but not Usenet newsgroups. Documents retrieved from a keyword search are ranked according to the number of search terms matched at once. The Lycos site touts the evaluative quality of much of its organization, presenting such resources as their "Top 5%" directory of best Web sites, and their choice of best online newspapers. Lycos offers subject-directory browsing for a general audience, with the primary categories being: News, Travel, Science, Culture, Business, Fashion, Sports, Technology, Education, Shopping, Entertainment, Government, Money, Health, Lifestyle, Kids, Careers, Autos. Additional resources include news wire services, city guides, and searchable databases of people and companies.

Open Text Index
   http://index.opentext.net/

The Open Text Index enables close control over search terms and the restriction of the search to Web document titles, summaries, URLs, first headings, or their entire texts. A very precise search can thus be made, but over a somewhat more limited scope (about two million Web pages). Usenet newsgroups, e-mail addresses, and "Current Events" (a dozen online newspapers) can also be searched.

Savvy Search
   http://guaraldi.cs.colostate.edu:2000

Savvy Search, an experimental search system developed in the Computer Science Department of Colorado State University, enables searches with several engines simultaneously. It is thus a powerful technique both for enabling a more or less comprehensive search of everything available on the Web concerning a specific topic, as well as comparing the characteristics of different search engines. (Researchers can link directly from this site to each of the Web search tools which Savvy Search queries.) Search term options include "all query terms" (i.e. Boolean AND), "as a phrase" (a "literal search") and "any query terms" (Boolean OR). Display options include the ability to "Integrate Results," which combines duplicate search results and does not separate them by search engine (the process does add 45 seconds to the time of the search, however). Savvy Search also has international language capabilities.

WWW Virtual Library
  http://www.w3.org/hypertext/DataSources/bySubject/Overview.html

A distributed subject catalog of Web resources. Primary divisions are into about 150 categories, including names of countries, areas of academic study (e.g. Asian Studies, Women's Studies), cultural forms (music, dance, theatre), scientific fields, and current issues (AIDS, environment). The resources are cross-classified by type of service (i.e. Web, Gopher, FTP, Telnet). Annotated links to other Internet search tools are provided.

WebCrawler
  http://Webcrawler.com/

WebCrawler was the first full-text search engine on the Internet (searching the full content of files, not just their titles). This powerful research tool began as a graduate student's research project at the University of Washington and was later sold to America Online and then to Excite, Inc. and became part of the Excite network of research tools. (Use of it remains free to the public.) WebCrawler's keyword search supports all the Boolean search operators (including NEAR and ADJ); if no operators are specified in a list of search terms, "OR" is the default (that is, WebCrawler will search for matches of any of the terms, in any combination). Results can be returned just as titles (for easier scanning), or with descriptions. A "relevance indicator" accompanies each term, scoring Web documents on the frequency and combination of search terms in them. WebCrawler provides an interactive map service for 22,000 U.S. cities. If your search terms include one of these cities (for example, "colleges in San Francisco"), the corresponding map is automatically offered among the search matches. WebCrawler also offers subject directories for browsing, with the following eighteen primary categories: Arts, Business, Chat, Computers, Education, Entertainment, Games, Health, Internet, Kids, Life, News, Recreation, Reference, Romance, Science, Sports, Travel.

Yahoo!
> *http://www.yahoo.com/*

One of the first search engines to offer extensive directories of links organized by subject, Yahoo remains an extremely powerful resource. Designed primarily for a general and popular audience, Yahoo organizes material initially into fourteen broadly-defined categories: Arts and Humanities, Business and Economy, Computers and Internet, Education, Entertainment, Government, Health, News and Media, Recreation and Sports, Reference, Regional, Science, Social Science, and Society and Culture. From each of these categories, the researcher selects more narrowly-defined subjects.

While Yahoo has been noted primarily for the depth of its subject directories, it also offers a powerful keyword search. Initially, the researcher has the option to search Usenet newsgroups, a directory of e-mail addresses, or Yahoo categories themselves (a useful first step to browsing the directories that are related to your research topic. When searching Yahoo make sure you carefully define the search area: "Yahoo categories" will search the names of directories themselves, while "Web Sites" will conduct a much broader search and retrieve specific Web pages related to your topic. Boolean search strings are supported; additionally, if you are looking only for very current material, you have the option to limit the search to listings added within a specified period of time—from one day to three years.

Saving the Product

In addition to familiarizing your students with the methods of organization in Gopherspace and on the Web, and teaching them about keyword searches and Boolean strings, there are other strategies for Internet browsing which can help make their work more productive.

Instruct your students about the basic principle that, especially with client software, whatever they are looking at can be easily downloaded and saved. With text files this is often as simple as choosing the "Save as..." command, which will save the material either onto the computer's hard drive or a student diskette. Depending on the browser they use, students will also have the option of saving graphic files, sound files and other media. Sometimes, the designer of a Gopherhost or a Web site will have programmed another method for downloading files—for example, clicking on the links of a Web page might download the item to your computer. Look for FAQ and "readme" files located on the specific sites for further information.

Downloading graphics, sound or video files will be most beneficial for your students if they are building multimedia projects. Downloading text files, however, is a productive method of research for a wider range of topics, including the "traditional" research paper. If there is a limit to the number of Internet-connected computers at your institution, downloading text files is especially useful—students can take these files and read them on any computer, freeing up the Internet-connected computer for research by other students. Advise your students about the need to be somewhat selective, however, and certainly to be critical readers of the materials they retrieve from Internet browsing.

Although the tremendous amount of material available on the Internet can be seductive, downloading everything about a particular topic may not be a viable search strategy. Students need to choose selectively in order for their research to be effective. However, because of the changing nature of the Internet, if they find a potentially useful resource, they should make sure to save a copy, as well as note the address of the site from which it came. (For information on documenting Internet sources see Appendix Three.)

Finally, you and your students should make use of bookmarks and hotlists. These lists contain the information for connecting directly to a particular site or document. They may be broad, taking the user to the opening window or home page of an institution, or narrow, taking the user directly to a specific document (the latter is especially common on the Web, where every file receives its own URL). Providing your students with a hotlist of useful sites can be a good way to introduce them to Gopher and the Web. With these lists students can connect to pre-selected sites merely by choosing a menu item. You might gather a list of sites and materials all pertaining to the topic of your course, or, if you are interested in your students designing Web pages (see Chapter Six), you might give them a hotlist of pages with interesting designs. As students spend more time browsing, they can develop lists of their own.

Introductory Exercises: Internet Browsing

• Introduce the organization of Gopherspace by having students tunnel to a specified site. • Introduce students to Boolean operators as a prelude to the different kinds of keyword searches; assign them a comparison of the results produced by different combinations of search terms. • If available, use your institution's electronic library catalog as a transition to concepts of online research. Students should be able to e-mail themselves the results of searches on the online catalog, reinforcing earlier Internet skills. • Have students practice browsing through subject trees to become familiar with their organizational techniques. Discuss with students the organizational logic of where particular information might be located. • Require students to use a diskette reserved for Internet research (as opposed to e-mail, Web-building projects, etc.); design an assignment which demonstrates the process of saving information from Web and Gopher research.

Sample Assignments

- As an introduction to Internet browsing, have your students participate in an online "scavenger hunt." Choose one or more subjects related to class issues and ask students to find and save five documents that relate to those topics by tunneling or surfing with either Gopher, or the Web. You can also use this assignment as an opportunity to show students how to compile bookmarks or hotlists while they are researching a topic. Once your students have made their bookmarks, you can create a useful class resource by compiling them.

- Have students run a series of keyword searches on a topic. Make sure that they try different types of searches, preferably using at least one search engine for both Gopher and the Web. This exercise can teach students how to narrow or broaden a keyword search in order to gather a reasonable number of "hits" for a research project. Work with Boolean commands, and stress the *process* of researching on the net.

- Perhaps as an intermediate stage in a research project, have students compare the types of sources they find in the library with the types of sources they find browsing in Gopherspace or on the Web. Ask them to assess the materials critically and suggest how each type might be usefully incorporated into their argument. Look carefully at the kinds of materials that might be found only online or only in a library. Have students evaluate the advantages and disadvantages of including both types of research.

BROWSING CASE STUDY
Discovering the Plight of the Yanomami

This case study makes use of some of the browsing techniques outlined earlier in the chapter to show the possibilities for doing research on the Internet. It begins with the typical situation of a
student with a topic that is too broad. While this case study follows
a progression from keyword searches, to browsing and tunneling, to
refined keyword searches, the best research techniques will depend a
great deal on the individual topics pursued by your students.

Perhaps even more so than when using traditional research sources,
students should focus their topics when searching on the net. Take,
for example, the case of a student who wanted to write on "the
environment":

```
ACADEMIC PERIODICAL INDEX -- TITLE KEYWORD
═══════════════════════════════════════════
Your search: ENVIRONMENT
matches 5373 items
```

Library catalog search results

environment   [Search]

Search Results
Top 25 of 73952 for **environment**
Show **summaries** for these results.

WebCrawler search results

The samples above compare a search done with a traditional library
catalog to one performed using the WebCrawler search engine on
the World Wide Web. Note that the library search (combing through

125

the extensive resources at the University of Texas) returned 5,373 items while the search of the Internet returned a whopping 73,952 "hits." In both cases, students must limit the scope of their search.

A student might begin limiting a search by using the Boolean operators offered by Veronica—in this case by specifying some other keyword to include with the search for the environment. Let's assume that the course has been studying "third world" and "first world" relations and the student is interested in the impact of these relations on the environment of the "third world." She might include "third world" in her search for the environment by using the key terms "environment and third world."

*** Your search on "environment and third world" returned nothing***

"Environment and third world" results

It hardly seems likely that there is no information on the Internet about the environment and the "third world"; these results demonstrate the need to be flexible when using keyword searches. When a search term does not return any items, a student might try a synonym or some related keywords to improve the results.

A SEED (Action for Solidarity, Equality, Environment

ISODE - The ISO Development Environment

48 out of 192 (get info here).

"Environment and development" results

Using the keywords "environment and development," the search has been narrowed and returns 192 items, a more manageable number of resources. Closer scrutiny of some of the entries would reveal, however, that many of the returns don't actually concern the "third world." For example, some of the entries refer to computer environments and software development. This is still too wide a focus for a key-word search seeking materials for a research paper. At this point, the student could try refining the keyword search by using the Boolean strategy of excluding a term, for example, entering "environment and development not computers." Part of the problem, however, may be that the student needs a more specific focus to drive the search. One strategy for refining the topic might be to scroll through the "environment and development" search returns to get a better sense of existing information on the Internet.

If the student is still narrowing the topic, however, she might also explore some of the Internet subject directories where information is stored. This can be accomplished in part by following the different branches of the many subject directories, or "trees," that can be accessed via Gopher or the Web.

Below is a sample from a browsing session utilizing a subject tree. Note that this example illustrates the ways that the Web has sub-sumed some of the functions of Gopher. Although the student initiated this search from the ElNet Galaxy Web site (*http://galaxy.einet.net/ GJ/subject-trees.html*), this particular subject tree is actually a Gopher directory.

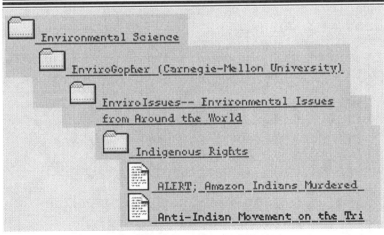

Tunnelling through a subject tree
127

The search begins with the general branch "Environmental Science," then digs down through various other subjects until it reaches the heading for indigenous rights. The directory, "Indigenous Rights," is contained by the "Environmental Issues from Around the World" directory and by the more general "Environmental Science" directory, so that the movement from "the environment" through "Environmental Issues from Around the World," parallels in some ways the refinements made to the keyword search. At the end of the subject tunnels, the student would find the article, "ALERT: Amazon Indians Murdered." Here's a sample from the article mentioned:

```
From: ACTIV-L via John Doe
<jd@boolean.cube.edu>
Subject: ALERT: Amazon Indians Murdered on
Protected Lands
Date: 25 Aug 1993 00:53:10 GMT
Also Posted to ACTIV-L and
misc.activism.progressive (by Somebody Else)
=======================================================
[additional headers deleted]

Brazil:

AMAZON INDIANS MURDERED ON PROTECTED LANDS
URGENT ACTION REQUESTED

On August 17, 1993, an entire village of
Yanomami Indians was found massacred in the
region of Homoxi-Xidea in the Brazilian
state of Roraima, Northern Amazon.  Reports
from the daily newspaper "Estado de Sao
Paulo" say that the number of dead is over
forty.  The massacre occurred within the
boundaries of the legally demarcated
Yanomami Park.... [remainder deleted]

Gopher://dolphin.envirolink.org:70/00/
.EnviroIssues/Indigenous%20Rights/
ALERT%3B_Amazon_Indians_Murdered_6-1-95
```

This excerpt represents some of the alternative sources of information that can be found using the Internet. Note that the article was first posted to the listserv ACTIV-L as well as to the newsgroup *misc.activism.progressive.* Many such postings are archived on the Internet and will turn up during subject-driven browsing or in keyword searches. The article is not a traditionally "published" source, but does seem to be carefully written and informative. Again, this type of reading foregrounds the need to exercise critical reading skills when using online research sources.

One other point should be made about the excerpt. After tunneling through several directory levels and scrolling through the entries for each, it is quite possible to lose track of where an article was found. In addition, an article available yesterday might be gone tomorrow. For these reasons, students should save articles as text files for later use. In this case, the student copied the location of the file and the date the article was found and pasted it at the bottom of the article. If the student finds this to be a valuable resource for her paper, the citation will be ready to use when she begins to compose. (For information about documenting Internet sources, see the citation guide in Appendix Three).

In addition to saving and documenting sources as part of the browsing process, we also recommend creating a bookmark for any sites which might be particularly useful. This is helpful when a site contains more articles than a student can deal with at any given time. With a bookmark, a student might also return to the site later to look for any updates to the material she has already examined.

After saving the article above, the student might browse through other subjects contained by "Environmental Issues from Around the World." In this tunneling session, the student was able to find, save, and document the following articles:

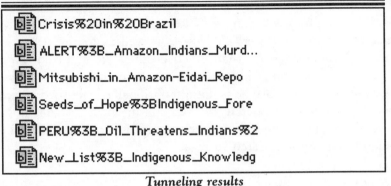

Tunneling results

Note that the final entry actually gives information about the forming of a listserv devoted to the topic of indigenous people. This is important because it highlights what we see as the intersection of research and conversation that takes place when working on the Internet. Instructors might want to think about beginning the research process early in the semester so that students can post queries and engage in discussion about the research topic on any pertinent newsgroups or mailing lists discovered during the research process.

📄	INDIGENOUS VIEWS OF LAND AND THE ENVIRONMENT
📄	-=- Indigenous people and the environment (fwd)
📄	Indigenous people and the environment
📄	Indigenous people and the environment (fwd)
📄	Endangered_Peoples_Indigenous_Rights_and_the_ Environment
📄	Indigenous Environment Systems (Ecology)
📁	10 out of 10 (get info here).

Veronica search for "indigenous and environment"

Let's assume that the student has now decided to focus on the impact of development on indigenous peoples. She might return to the keyword searching process with this new focus and look for resources more specific to her interests. To receive the results from the example above, the student performed a new Veronica search using the keywords "indigenous and environment." The sample graphic has been edited, but note that the 192 hits from the earlier "environment and development" search have been reduced to just ten. A similar reduction occurs when the student searches for "indigenous and development":

```
📄 Zabin, C.A. (1989) "Grassroots Development in Indig
📄 Indigenous ecological knowledge and development of t
📄 Indigenous knowledge and development: An ideological
📄 Indigenous knowledge, biodiversity conservation, and
📄 Indigenous farming systems and development of tropic
📁 Center for Indigenous Knowledge in Agriculture & Rur
📄 Indigenous forest dwellers in forest development pla
📁 15 out of 15 (get info here).
```

Veronica search for "indigenous and development"

The twenty-five items returned from the last two searches together make a manageable list of possible resources for the student's interests. Note that the list of items returned from a Gopher search can sometimes be misleading. Many times an item may be listed more than once, or a listing might provide a review rather than the actual text of a book or article. The many book reviews online reveal a way to incorporate Internet research with traditional work in the library. One of the Gopher entries, for, example, reads:

131

> Babbitt, B., 1992. Gold rush brings cultural
> clash to Amazon region. Forum for Applied
> Research and Public Policy 7(4):5-12.
>
> Discusses the devasting effect of the gold
> rush on the Yanomani Indians who live in the
> Brazilian rain forests.

The entry in fact points the student to a potentially useful article that might be found in the library. Note that the review for the published source contains mechanical errors and even spells the Yanomami name incorrectly. This does not, of course, reflect on the published article, but again highlights the need for close evaluation of all our sources.

It will also be useful to try looking for the same information using some of the other Internet research tools, namely keyword searches on the World Wide Web. Even when performing keyword searches, students will find that gathering resources on the Web is a more fluid process than using Gopher. For example, the student who continued her search for the keywords "indigenous and environment" on the Web might receive these results.

WebCrawler Search Results

The query "indigenous and environment" found 40

1000 ftp://ftp.halcyon.com/pub/FWDP/Internation
0398 People of the Rainforest
0235 FWDP -- North, Central and South American
0195 Hot-Topics at IR/PS
0110 http://www.wssd.apc.org/aa5mar.txt

Web search for "indigenous and environment"

This search (performed using the WebCrawler search engine) returns a list of items containing one of the keywords. Some of the items listed, however, may be other sites on the Web which are devoted to the topic. If the student followed the link to the "People of the Rainforest," for example, she would come across a Web site operated by a middle school in Washington State. From this site, she would find a link to the Fourth World Documentation Project's home page (*http://www.halcyon.com/FWDP/fwdp.html*) and from there a link to a searchable database with a number of documents about indigenous people. Sometimes this path of links can be hard to replicate (and, of course, sites may change) so, again, use bookmarks, hotlists or other navigational aids to make saving and documenting useful articles part of the process of browsing.

Before we end, let's imagine for a minute that the student decided to focus her project on one of the items that turned up during her subject tree browsing, the plight of the Yanomami in the Amazon. Hopefully the resources that she has found concerning larger issues of development and indigenous peoples will provide enough background information to contextualize the topic. Next, she may want to search the Web sites that she has been exploring for specific information about the Yanomami. A WAIS search of the Fourth World Documentation Project's database, for example, would return:

```
yanomami.txt
        Score: 1000, Lines: 272, Bytes: 13258
costrica.txt
        Score: 603, Lines: 392, Bytes: 20804
00_INDEX.AMERICAS
        Score: 594, Lines: 326, Bytes: 22000
icsa.txt
        Score: 218, Lines: 1255, Bytes: 53568
```

Yanomami search from a Web site

At this point, the student might decide she needs more specific resources to add depth to her chosen topic. Returning to Gopher and performing a Veronica search for "Yanomami" would return:

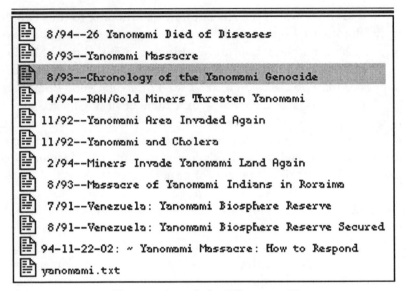

8/94--26 Yanomami Died of Diseases

8/93--Yanomami Massacre

8/93--Chronology of the Yanomami Genocide

4/94--RAN/Gold Miners Threaten Yanomami

11/92--Yanomami Area Invaded Again

11/92--Yanomami and Cholera

2/94--Miners Invade Yanomami Land Again

8/93--Massacre of Yanomami Indians in Roraima

7/91--Venezuela: Yanomami Biosphere Reserve

8/91--Venezuela: Yanomami Biosphere Reserve Secured

94-11-22-02: ~ Yanomami Massacre: How to Respond

yanomami.txt

Veronica search for "Yanomami"

Again, not all of these entries are likely to be useful "articles" and the student will probably want to supplement these resources with traditional items from the library, as well as consider some of the more general resources discovered in prior searches. She may want to read some of the materials before refining her search even further, and she should certainly consider participating in any of the newsgroups and listservs turned up during the research process, especially after having developed enough knowledge of the topic to pose a useful query. Whatever further steps she takes, she should be well on the way toward gathering enough resources to produce an in-depth project. Here's a sampling of some of the items found while preparing this case:

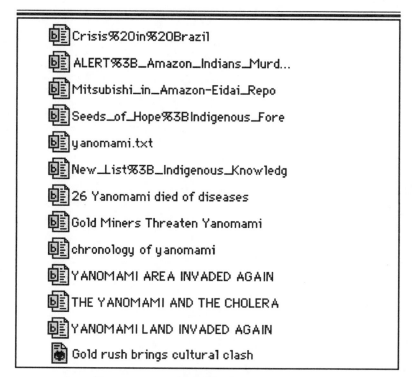

Documents gathered by browsing the net

Note that a keyword search of a library catalog for articles on the Yanomami returned fourteen items; just one more than the final results of our Internet browsing. If the student makes use of both of these kinds of resources, she can solidify the documentation of her project with additional library sources, and she can add both depth and currency to her understanding of the topic by browsing the Internet.

Chapter Five: Browsing the Net

Chapter Six
Node Construction Ahead: 6
The Web and Hypertext
Markup Language

WHAT IS HTML?_____

In Chapter Five, we examined how students can benefit from browsing the World Wide Web for research materials. In this chapter, we discuss the fundamentals of a deeper level of Web interaction: the building of Web pages using Hypertext Markup Language (HTML). As we stated in the previous chapter, the Web represents a convergence of hypertext, multimedia, and Internet connectivity (subsuming in the process many of the functions of earlier Internet media). As a result, the Web is a powerful new medium for the presentation of ideas, a fact visible in its exponential growth. We hope to demonstrate the pedagogical value of Web building as a new form of writing. In doing so, we will discuss the fundamentals of building as well as the rhetorical considerations crucial for a smooth integration of this new medium into the composition classroom.

Some elements of the spatial makeup of the Web were discussed in the previous chapter: that every Web page has its own particular address (called a URL), that pages are grouped together in sites produced by a single user or organization, that these groups of pages reside on Web servers, and that the movement from page to page is a fluid one. In this chapter, you will learn how to produce Web pages and upload them to a server so that they can be viewed by the Internet-connected world. The process of HTML scripting is surprisingly easy and can be learned in multiple stages. Students can produce interesting, attractive documents with only the most fundamental commands, adding more sophisticated elements as their knowledge increases.

One of the first concepts that Web builders should understand is the basic relationship between a Web page and its underlying HTML script. Say you were looking at the page below with a Web browser:

Looking at the same example with a text editor would reveal the HTML script:

```
This will be normal text
<HR>
<B>This will be bold</B>
```

In HTML, a pair of bracketed tags like <B> . . . </B> instruct the browser to format the text between the commands. The tags, together with the text that they format, are called an HTML "element." Some additional elements which affect the layout of the page do not have like an ending tag, such as the <HR> ("horizontal rule") element. These are called "empty" elements.

In this chapter, we explore the rhetorical significance of publishing Web pages, looking especially at the challenge of creating effective multimedia hypertext documents. We discuss the process of teaching your class HTML commands and consider the organizational strategies needed to work successfully on the Web. Finally, our Case Study examines the development of a class Web site containing extensive student work with HTML.

Key Terms

Form: mechanism by which Web browsers allow users to send information back to the server. Forms can be used in a writing class to facilitate interaction between readers and authors of Web documents.

Home Page: conventional name given to a site on the World Wide Web. This name can be used for the central page of both a university or business site and for the personal page of an individual.

HTML (Hypertext Markup Language): the scripting language which is used to turn plain text and other elements (such as images) into the integrated pages we see on the Web.

Hypertexts: interactive documents that allow users to follow links to other documents and to present images, sound, and video.

Imagemap: an image which has been "mapped" by HTML commands so that clicking on different portions of it will link the user to different sites or files.

Index Page: the initial page of a site (or of a series of documents) which provides the organizational structure that maps the site—often the "starting point" for a hypertext.

Inline Image: an image which has been inserted into the design of a Web page.

> **Link:** a hypertextual function that connects documents, sites, and other media. Note that "link" is commonly used both as a noun to indicate the actual connection between one node and another, and as a verb to indicate the process by which this connection is achieved.
>
> **Node:** a hypertextual site which organizes multiple links. Nodes can contain any combination of text, links, graphics, sound, and video.
>
> **URL (Uniform Resource Locator):** the address assigned to each file on the World Wide Web.
>
> **Web Browser:** client software used for navigating and interacting with the World Wide Web. The Web browser translates the HTML source documents that reside on the Web into a fluid, multimedia interface.
>
> **Web Server:** a server equipped with software to facilitate the Hypertext Transfer Protocol (HTTP) that enables documents to be linked and shared on the Web. Users can access the documents stored on Web servers with a Web browser.
>
> **World Wide Web:** abbreviated *WWW* or *the Web*. Distributed hypermedia system built upon older protocols (FTP, Gopher, etc.) and additional newer protocols (HTTP). WWW client software provides the ability to view many types of files (HTML, GIF, text, etc.).

WHY USE HTML?

Publishing for an Electronic Audience

The unique potential of HTML as a simple medium for distributing multimedia texts allows students to structure their writing for presentation to a larger readership. While newsgroups, e-mail and MU*s all allow students to develop compositions for Internet audiences,

HTML documents can be much more polished, extensive, and complicated productions that link together different sources of information and media, much like a print publication.

Students composing in HTML know that their work will be seen by any number of people, and that the level of sophistication and polish will directly impact the way their work is received. Faced with these absent and potentially critical readers, students respond with a heightened awareness of the need to shape their pages for consumption.

We should note, however, that one of the struggles for a teacher using HTML is the tension arising from the general lack of quality of existing models of composition on the Web. Stressing to your students that their writing is to be held to a higher standard than most sites on the Web can be a difficult task when students come across more commercial order forms than accomplished arguments. Still, viewing Web construction as publication (with a permanence and expanded readership analogous to traditional print publishing) can be motivational for students.

You can use the prospect of publishing student work as an opportunity to discuss the importance of revision—both a close reading to make sure everything in their project is mechanically polished, as well as a chance to revise and refine their argumentation for a larger audience. If you have your students complete their projects locally before they are published (as we explain later), revision doesn't have to stop with the first publication of student work. The inclusion of a comment form or the author's e-mail address provides a simple way for readers to respond to a published Web page. Students interested and committed to their projects will take these critiques into account and incorporate them into further revisions.

Publishing as a Resource

Major class projects are easily archived on the Web because they are put in a "permanent" location on a server when they are published.

141

For those with Web capabilities, HTML offers access to class materials for almost all operating systems. Thus readers with either Mac, PC or Unix machines can examine student Web projects, and students with either Macs or PCs at home can work on their Web compositions.

As an even more ambitious project, an instructor may want to document the entire activity of a course by publishing (or having students publish) course materials like syllabi, policy statements, readings, assignments, student work, and, perhaps, weekly summaries of class events. In addition, documenting class activity and including transcripts of online class discussion is an excellent way to highlight the development of important class themes, and to discover connections between them. During the course, the class site can become an important resource for students, both as a means to catch up on what they might have missed, and as a way to reexamine and reevaluate the content of the course. After the course, the site can be an important means of evaluating different assignments and pedagogical strategies. Archiving class materials on the Web also enables instructors of different classes or at different institutions to tap the potentials of distance learning.

New Forums, New Forms

The ease with which multimedia, especially graphics, are incorporated into Web pages allows instructors to emphasize the rhetorical issues surrounding the use of these media in argumentation. The initial temptation is to overload a page with pictures, employing the graphical capabilities of HTML simply because they are new and exciting. As a countermeasure, instructors should highlight the rhetorical connections between the text and media on a page. Like a successfully integrated quotation, effective images are contextualized and related to relevant points of a student argument. Images should add another level of understanding to a work rather than confuse or distract a reader.

The most pronounced feature of HTML, the ability to link to any number of documents on Web servers around the world, makes the need for well-contextualized connections even more important. Whether they are linking to another section of their own argument or to a remote site, students should explain why they are providing the links and what the reader can expect to find by following the links.

Similarly, composing with links, texts, and media helps students to see that the resources they use are an essential part of argumentation, rather than items to be listed on a works cited page. This is particularly true since Web resources can be downloaded and then incorporated, edited, or "borrowed" by student writers. By examining and testing these materials, students can incorporate the ideas of other Web designers into their compositions, thereby highlighting the way that the production of knowledge is a communal process, but also raising concerns about intellectual property and plagiarism (see Appendix Two for information on copyright issues).

We also want to stress that placing student writing in the public domain raises unresolved legal and ethical concerns. We recommend having students sign a waiver granting the instructor permission to publish their projects both during the course and as a long-term archival resource.

HOW CAN YOUR CLASS USE HTML?_____

Working With New Materials

Successful Web building first requires some knowledge of the organizational structures of Web projects and an understanding of the relationship between Web pages as viewed through a browser, and the underlying HTML scripts. Before students begin to build, we recommend that they browse the Web in search of sites with interesting hypertextual designs. Remember that the linear model of composition presented by the traditional paper does not translate directly to the Web medium. Traditional papers can be posted on the Web by adding the necessary HTML formatting commands, but the Web audience is likely to skip long pages of scrollable text in favor of sites that incorporate graphics and offer more opportunity for the reader to interact. These expectations for Web pages can be critiqued as a sign of a more superficial presentation of information, but an emphasis on bells and whistles, on delivering nonlinear information with the help of new media, need not preclude critical thinking.

HTML Writers and Helper Applications

Working with Web pages, more than any other Internet activity discussed in this book, requires a variety of programs. Check with your systems administrator about which programs your institution supports. In addition to a browser for viewing and navigating the Web, you will need:

- A text editor or word processor to compose your HTML files. While you can compose HTML with any word processor, we recommend using an HTML editor which will automate many of the scripting commands and offer other useful features.

- An FTP client to upload your files to a Web server so that browsers can access them. (See Appendix Four for information on FTP.)

- Helper applications to open graphic, sound and video files as well as to handle more advanced browser functions. These applications can vary greatly and should be coordinated with your Web browser and your workstation's capacity.

144

Viewing the Source

One way to initiate the Web building process is by using the HTML viewing functions of most browsers to look at the underlying HTML document that organizes a particular Web page. In most browsers this is done with a menu command, such as "View Source." Initiating the view source function downloads a copy of the HTML file and opens it in a text editor so that students can see the different HTML commands that were used to make the page:

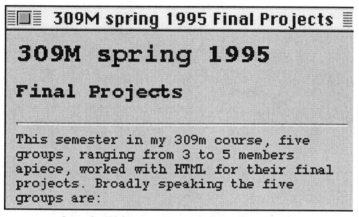

Sample Web page viewed through a browser

Viewing the source for the above page would reveal the HTML commands that control the format of the document:

```
<TITLE>309M spring 1995 Final Projects</TITLE>
<H1>309M spring 1995</H1>
<H2>Final Projects</H2>
<HR>This semester in my 309M course, five
groups, ranging from 3 to 5 members apiece,
worked with HTML for their final projects.
Broadly speaking the five groups are:
```

As a conceptual beginning, students should understand that Web building takes place in this underlying HTML document. By viewing the source, we can demonstrate this relationship. Note how the

145

sample from the browser has the title in the window bar at the top of the page "309M spring 1995 Final Projects." Looking at the source document reveals the command that places that information in the window bar:

```
<TITLE>309M spring 1995 Final Projects</TITLE>
```

The same holds true for the headings, the larger text that begins the document proper:

```
<H1>309M spring 1995 </H1>
<H2>Final Projects</H2>
<HR>This semester in my 309M course...
```

The largest heading in the sample "309M spring 1995" is controlled by the <H1> . . . </H1> element. HTML offers six heading levels, with <H1> being the largest and <H6> the smallest. Between the headings and the body text, a line is drawn across the top of the browser page by using the horizontal rule element, <HR>.

HTML Basics

The source document above can also serve as our introduction to HTML. The first thing to note is that HTML commands are all designated with bracketed tags using the less-than and greater-than signs, <>. We should also note that the sample demonstrates the two major types of HTML commands. The first type of HTML command works in pairs. Note how the <TITLE> element begins with an opening tag, is followed by the information on which the command is going to operate (in this case the text "309M spring 1995 Final Projects") and concludes with the second part of the bracketed pair, the closing tag </TITLE>. This <command> . . . </command> form is the most common command structure in HTML scripting.

The second type of HTML command shown in the sample is the "empty" element, self-contained within a single set of brackets. In

146

this sample it is the <HR> command, which tells a browser to draw a line (horizontal rule) across the screen. Three of the most common single-element commands used to control the appearance of Web pages are the horizontal rule command, the paragraph break <P>, and the line break <BR>. These formatting elements are inserted into the HTML document in order to keep the text from running together when viewed by a Web browser.

Images and Links

Keeping the distinction between different kinds of HTML elements in mind can help us understand two slightly more complex HTML commands, namely images and links:

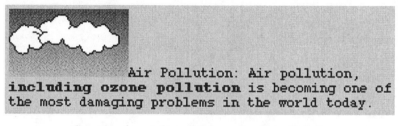

Sample of an inline image and a textual link

(Note that the linked text, "including ozone pollution" appears in boldface in the sample, but would also be set off with colored text in most browsers)

Viewing the source of the sample above would reveal

```
<IMG ALIGN=bottom SRC="clouds.gif"> Air Pol-
lution: Air pollution,
<A HREF="http://www.greenpeace.org/~ozone/">
including ozone pollution</A> is becoming one
of the most damaging problems in the world
today.
```

The first element from this sample, the inline image, works like a formatting command by using a single set of brackets.

```
<IMG ALIGN=bottom SRC="clouds.gif">
```

Within those brackets, additional information is provided. The inline image element <IMG> is followed by attributes specifying the layout of any subsequent text in relationship to the image (ALIGN=bottom). Within the command there is also information about the name and source of the image (SRC="clouds.gif"). The "SRC=" attribute tells the browser where to find the image and can include an entire URL if the image does not reside in the same file system as the HTML document. In this case, the browser is told to find the image "clouds.gif" (which is in the same directory local file system), to place the image in the Web page and to align any text which comes after it at the bottom of the image.

A Sample URL

Recall that every file on the Web has a unique address or URL. The sample above demonstrates both a local and a remote URL. The source for the inline image is a local file.

SRC="clouds.gif"

Thus the file name, "clouds.gif," serves as the local URL.

The sample address following the <A HREF> element utilizes a remote URL.

http://www.greenpeace.org/~ozone/

Unlike the local URL, the entire address must be given, since this file is located on a different Web server.

The sample also illustrates the basics of the HTML link command. In this case, the command provides additional information but works with paired brackets to designate the hot text, or anchor, for the link:

```
<A HREF="http://www.greenpeace.org/~ozone/"> including
ozone pollution</A>
```

The information that is given in the opening tag indicates that an anchor for a link is being established and gives a reference which tells the browser what to do when someone clicks on the hot text. In this case, the browser is told to go to a page sponsored by Greenpeace with information about ozone and the environment. The entire URL is specified, which will send the reader to the page: *http://www.greenpeace.org/~ozone/*. All of this information is contained within the first set of brackets that makes up the command. The ending tag </A> merely works to close the command. As with the <TITLE> element, everything in between the two sets of brackets will be acted upon by the command. In this case, the phrase "including ozone pollution" will become hot text when viewed by a browser, and clicking on the phrase will activate the link to Greenpeace.

These commands are given merely to illustrate the basic functioning of HTML. This section is not intended as a complete list of all HTML possibilities. For more information about specific HTML commands, see Appendix Seven on HTML commands, or look for the tutorials and resources at, among others, The HTML Documentation Site (*http://www.utoronto.ca/Webdocs/HTMLdocs/NewHTML/htmlindex.html*), and at the Yahoo HTML site (*http://www.yahoo.com/Computers/World_Wide_Web/HTML/*). There are also many HTML editors (available by FTP as freeware) which automate the process of composing in HTML. Whether you use an HTML editor or not, however, your students should understand the basic structure of these commands so they can check the HTML information when a link or image is not working, or when a page needs modification.

Building Locally

The process of revising Web pages differs from that found in traditional composition. Students will need to move continually back and forth between the HTML document and the browser in order to see how their page is being displayed. For this reason, you will want to teach students the process of making changes to their HTML files and then "reloading" their revised documents in a browser. To facilitate this composition process, students should build their files within single folders or directories on a diskette or local hard drive, rather than on the Web server where they will eventually reside.

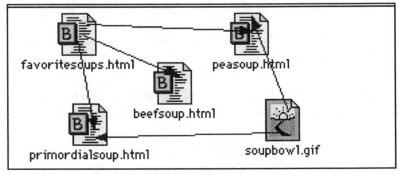

Files in a local directory

The sample above shows several different files which all exist within a single directory, or folder. Note that the project makes use of both HTML files and graphics files, as designated by the *.html* and *.gif* suffixes on their file names, respectively. On the Web, the major types of files are HTML documents (.html), text files (.txt), graphics files (.gif) and (.jpeg), movie files (.mpeg) and (.mov), and sound files (.wav) and (.au). In order for browsers to read files they must be named with the proper suffixes. File names in a PC format will use the shortened three character suffixes: (.htm), (.jpg), and (.mpg). Note also that this sample uses all lowercase characters with no spaces between them in its file names. This strategy is important because some servers handle spaces and uppercase file names differently. While some browsers and situations are more forgiving, Web links are case-sensitive. For this reason, we strongly recommend that you have your students use all lowercase characters with no spaces between them in both their file names and their HTML links. This convention will save a lot of time when uncovering typographical mistakes which cause broken links.

Logistically, local files simplify Web building a great deal. An early exercise in making links, for example, is much simpler if a student can enter the name of a local file without a lengthy URL. Building locally also allows students to easily revise their projects as part of the composition process. In addition, instructors will likely find that organizing HTML projects is much less troublesome when small groups or individuals are responsible for the management of their own files. Building locally will also make things easier when moving files to your Web server; if all of the links work within a directory on a local level, then the links should continue to work regardless of their final position on a server.

Serving it Up

Organizing your files and uploading them to a server will require some extra time and energy, especially if you are uncomfortable with the various technologies. Whatever your level of technological knowledge, we recommend that you coordinate with your Web administrators as you work through the various tasks involved in serving your files.

We have outlined the way that Web compositions exist as both the displayed page seen through a browser and the HTML documents which organize that display. While most of the building will take place on the level of HTML files, an instructor needs to understand one additional aspect of Web building, namely the "serving" of the Web documents. Serving files involves two major activities: 1) overseeing the behind-the-scenes operations of the Web server, including setting up form and imagemap routines, and running software which provides the proper protocol for sharing files on the Web, and 2) managing directory structures and files which reside on the Web server.

Usually your computation center or some other institutional entity will be responsible for the behind-the-scenes operations of the Web server, so most instructors will probably not be involved in the first of these two activities (if you need information about the server-side operations of the Web, see *http://Web66.coled.umn.edu/Cookbook/*). The one area of server expertise that you will need to have is directory and file management. Some institutions will provide students with individual accounts for Web building, but in many cases, the instructor will be responsible for managing files for the entire class. This can involve a considerable amount of work, and is one of the reasons that we strongly recommend that students use all lowercase characters without spaces in their file names. Uniformity simplifies the file management process tremendously.

Before considering the ways that you might upload finished files to the server, you should think about the directory structures that will house those files. If you are familiar with directories in DOS or with a folder filing system in either Windows or Macintosh, then you will be fairly comfortable with the organization of Web files. Rather than uploading all your files into a single directory, we suggest that you first organize your server space by making subdirectories. If you are teaching two or more classes, for example, you might provide a directory for each of them and, within those directories, you might make additional subdirectories for student projects, home pages and class resources. The organization will depend on your own needs, but considering these structures early in the building process will save you considerable time and effort in the long run.

Finally, you will need to upload the finished files to the server, most likely using an FTP client (see Appendix Four). If you had your students build local files (see "Building Locally" above), you may be able to load all of their directories at once, depending upon your FTP

HTML in the Classroom: Step-by-Step

1. Well before the start of the school term, explore the details of Web building at your institution: how much storage space will you have, and on what server? are complex functions like HTML forms, imagemaps, and message forums supported? what helper applications (browser, HTML editor, FTP client) are recommended?
2. Learn the process of uploading files to your Web server.
3. Before the start of the term, establish a site to document the activity of your courses. Post syllabi and assignment descriptions, create index pages to which student projects will later be linked, and set up message forums.
4. Early in the term, familiarize students with the relationship between a Web page and its HTML source document. Encourage students to browse the Web for pages with pleasing design features, and view their source documents to learn how these features are achieved.
5. Have students sign a waiver to publish on the Web the projects they will later complete. Discuss openly the implications of this waiver.
6. Stress that student writing will be held to a higher standard than much of what is found on the Web.
7. Throughout the first half of the term, give simple text-only Web building assignments to acquaint students with the basics of HTML scripting. Have students build locally (see p. 150), learning to link files to one another without worrying yet about the content of the files.
8. Discuss stylistic techniques of HTML (see p. 159), with liberal examples from the Web.
9. Gradually increase the complexity of HTML assignments, including some collaborative work. Have students post "draft" versions of their projects to the Web, making use of comment forms for peer (and public) feedback.

client. Otherwise, you will need to place files on the server individually. In any case, check that the final organization of the directories and files that you load to the server mirrors the structure of any projects developed locally. Additionally, when loading files, make sure that HTML documents and any text files are sent as "ASCII text" or "text only" and that other media are transported as "binary" or "raw data." Make sure that file names remain unaltered during the uploading process (turn off the feature on some FTP clients that appends suffixes to files as they are uploaded). Finally, after you have placed files on the server, you should check the links with a browser to ensure that nothing has gone wrong.

Weaving a Web Composition

Despite the strange appearance of some of the link and image elements above, we think you will find that students have little trouble with HTML scripting. There are a finite number of elements and attributes, and once students are comfortable with the process of building HTML documents with a text editor and viewing them with a browser, the composition itself goes quite smoothly. More important for the success of Web compositions may be the way that the organization of the project works to further the student's rhetorical goals.

Because of the hypertextual nature of the Web, the major themes of a composition or the strands of an argument can be organized as several different nodes of a project. When planning their documents, students should consider the potential paths that a reader might take to reach these nodes. The index page (the initial page which organizes a Web site, usually named "index.html") is in some ways analogous to the topic paragraph of a traditional essay. This page can be used to map out the direction of the project and to give the reader enough information to make informed choices about the possibilities for reading the document. Since Web projects can sometimes turn into long lists of unexplained links, instructors may want to have students map out their ideas on paper before composing their initial page.

Since the initial page of a Web site determines to a great extent the paths that a reader might take through a student project, this page should be organized so that it works to further the student's argument. If, for example, the student were to develop in detail one of the major claims of an argument by using a sub-node that must be accessed by following a link from the initial page, he should emphasize that link in such a way that readers will know to follow it if they are having questions about that claim.

If an idea is crucial to the argument, the author should assure that it gets developed either initially or with repetition at the various sub-nodes that rely on the idea. Students should not develop nodes under the assumption that a reader has understood information from (or even visited) a previous node. Instead, they should contextualize each node in such a way that a reader will be oriented to the argument of the project in general. These kinds of transitional reiterations are necessary in the Web medium and also can be useful tools for discussing coherence in general.

Imagemaps and Graphical Links

One way to maximize the organizational potential of a Web site is to incorporate the use of imagemaps into their layout. An imagemap is

Sample imagemap

155

a graphic image that has been set up to provide links to different areas of a Web site. Students configure "hot spots" on the image and a reader who clicks on one of the hot spots will be sent to whatever link has been assigned to that spot

The sample above uses a composite image to link to the major nodes of a project. These maps can be useful as they provide a quick visual navigational tool for the site. We should caution that not all servers support imagemaps, and configuring the hot spots and links is somewhat sophisticated. Check with your server administrator before deciding to use imagemaps (for more information about making imagemaps, see *http://www.utoronto.ca/Webdocs/HTMLdocs/ NewHTML/serv-ismap.html*).

You do not need to use an image map to add graphical links to your Web site. By placing an image in a Web page (see below) and then creating a link from that image, a student can design a site that uses visual elements to facilitate a reader's movement, without having to learn the complex operation of imagemaps. We recommend that small images be used to make links and that the student consider images that convey a sense of the link to be followed; a small picture of a house, for example, could be used to indicate a return link to the home page.

Working With Graphics

Depending on your facilities, you will likely have several options when it comes to using graphics on the Web. If you have graphics programs it will be possible to create your own images or to manipulate existing images for use on the Web. If not, then you can use some of the many images that have been made available at various sites around the Web. There are large archives of images available at most Web design sites and these may be freely incorporated into your pages. If you have storage space considerations, you can also use the URL of an image that exists somewhere else on the Web in your own documents. Linking to an image on another site will display that image in your own Web page. Most Web sites are fairly liberal about the use of their images, but you should investigate site policies and respect the considerations of intellectual property when linking to or downloading images from around the Web (see Appendix Two for more information on copyright considerations). A good policy is to ask permission with an e-mail message whenever you duplicate an image or link to a site.

Once you have appropriate graphics, you should consider the most effective way of incorporating them into your pages. First, the relatively large size of some images can make viewing Web pages frustrating, especially if a reader is using a modem to access your site. We recommend that inline images be less than thirty kilobytes (30K); you should link to larger images as separate files, providing descriptions and a clear indication of their sizes. You may also want to supply a reduced version of the image so that readers can glance at larger graphics without taking the time to download each one. Overloading a page, even with small images, can make viewing difficult as browsers must continually return to the server to load image after image. Additionally, some users do not have inline image functions and others disable the function on their browsers, so students should use the "ALT" attribute in their image elements (for example, <IMG ALIGN=bottom SRC="clouds.gif" ALT= "a picture of clouds">). The "ALT" option will display a textual alternative if a browser is unable to load an image.

Along with the logistical considerations involved in using graphics on the Web, students should consider the aesthetic impact of images in their compositions. One helpful suggestion is to think of the "screen full" as the rhetorical unit of Web compositions. A student who places an eight by ten inch graphic at the top of her Web page will have little room for anything else. While some situations may call for an entirely graphical page, we think that a combination of text and graphics makes best use of the Web's multimedia potential. A very large graphic leaves no room for text to converse with the image, to contextualize it, or to introduce the page.

Students should also be aware of a tendency for images to produce a false sense of explication. If students are using images as integral parts of their arguments (for example, using movie stills to evaluate aspects of a film), then they should accompany their graphics with a textual explication that makes clear connections between the images and the larger themes of the project.

Most important to remember is that images should not be used unnecessarily; they should strive to fulfill the rhetorical aims of the project. At the same time, keep in mind that the Web is a graphical environment. The audience for Web pages often expects something more than plain text, and students establish credible Web ethos by incorporating images into their pages, even if those images are only the various balls, colored lines, and other icons commonly found throughout the Web.

Using Forms to Interact with a Web Audience

If at all possible, we recommend that you have students include a comment form with each of their Web projects. Most comment forms are configured to send e-mail to the author of a Web page.

Your real name (optional):

Bozo Jones

Your message:

This project is very interesting, although there is a typo in the first paragraph. I think if you make the point about animal rights earlier it wil

Ship it   Reset this form

Sample comment form

By using interactive comment forms, you and your students can engage the global audience that the Web provides and utilize their collective expertise. As with imagemaps, the ability to use interactive forms will depend upon the capacities of your Web server. Check with your server administrator about the necessary components of forms, such as Java scripting and Common Gateway Interfaces (CGIs). Many browsers now support the HTML element <MAILTO>, which can be configured to send e-mail to an author. If your server does not support forms, you should consider having students include a <MAILTO> option in their pages to facilitate contact.

While the sample above shows the most basic contact form, you can modify forms to include fields for other information. (For more on forms, see *http://www.yahoo.com/Computers/World_Wide_Web/Programming/Forms/*). If you wanted students to offer peer-reviews of each other's pages, for example, you could include several prompts in the form to which students would respond. Forms can also be used by the instructor to send feedback about the project. Finally, forms offer the possibility that students may be contacted by someone outside the classroom about their work. We have found that the feedback gathered through forms can further the highly motivational aspects of publishing on the Web. To maximize this potential, submit your URL to some of the large database sites around the Web, circulate your URL on relevant listservs and newsgroups, and announce it to various site administrators so that they can provide links to your pages. The sprawling nature of the Web makes publicizing your pages a task that goes hand in hand with carefully constructing them.

Style Conventions on the Web

Although the Web is a medium that for the most part remains uncharted, some stylistic axioms are already beginning to be formulated. As we discussed above, one of the elements of good Web design involves the careful use of graphics. Overwhelming a reader with images or bogging down a system with large graphic files can constitute bad style. Some observers also feel that graphics should not be any wider than the standard size of a browsing window (about 6.75 inches).

Another stylistic axiom concerns the use of navigational links. The author should provide the reader with links to previous pages and to other relevant sections of the project. Usually navigational links are at the bottom of the page, though the document itself may dictate their placement.

Authors should also sign and date their Web pages. Again, most authors put this information at the bottom of the page. We recommend incorporating a contact function into an author's signature. This can be done by either providing a link to a comment form or by using the <MAILTO> command. Because readers will sometimes return to a site periodically to see if any new materials have been added, the page should also include the date of the last revision.

Finally, students should think carefully about the language that they use to make links in their documents. For example, the convention of using the phrase "click here" as hot text fails to convey any information about the link. A better implementation of hot text will emphasize a phrase that clearly describes the link to the reader.

While these general recommendations are important, we'd like to suggest that HTML style is not yet a well-defined, homogenous set of conventions. As the Web evolves, it will likely be put to a variety of new rhetorical purposes, and each of these will present its own demands and stylistic choices.

Introductory Exercises: HTML

- Establish a Web site for the course, and assign students the task of translating written work to html and posting it, as well as taking part in discussion through reply forms or a message forum (consider a portfolio system to grade Web site postings). • Give students an early assignment using the "View Source" function to compare several finished Web pages with their source documents. • On early building assignments, focus on hypertextual structure rather than the content of files, showing students how to link files locally within folders. • Develop "visual literacy" by giving students an assignment to gather, then discuss, images for potential use in a Web project. • To reinforce the organizational possibilities of hypertext as a prelude to a major Web-building project, have students (including collaborative groups) map out their ideas on paper, with revisions.

Sample Assignments

- Have students browse the Web and compile a hotlist of URLs related to a topic of study. After gathering a list of related sites, students can build a topic page which links to each of these sites. Students should avoid creating a long list of links; rather, they should give a brief description of what the reader might expect to find at each site.

- Have a small group of students construct a Web page about a text or topic. Assign various tasks to individual students and have them link their work to a central page. The group can also include links to useful URLs in their topic page and a credits or contact page to gather feedback about the project.

- Have students annotate a class text with HTML links. These links can either lead to other related texts or sites, or can be used to link to student explications of the text. After linking to various resources, use the annotated text as a resource for further study.

- Starting early in the semester, establish a class home page. Use the page to disseminate useful information about the class (for example, paper topics or syllabus updates). As students complete their regular assignments, use the class Web site to compile student papers and analyses and use these materials as resources for further study. Finally, make links from the class site to any Web projects undertaken by the students.

Chapter Six: HTML and Web Composition

HTML CASE STUDY

E316K Masterworks of American Literature
Instructor: Daniel Anderson
http://www.en.utexas.edu/~daniel/amlit/amlit.html

As we discuss throughout this chapter, building class-related Web pages with HTML is a relatively simple process, and yet it is a process which offers an enormous range of practical applications for both students and instructors. This case study examines a site which was developed as part of an American Literature survey held during the spring semester of 1995 at the University of Texas at Austin. We will look closely at the organization of the entire site and at individual student compositions.

Although this case study focuses on a class site devoted to literature rather than composition, we chose this example because it is an excellent representation of the many benefits that HTML scripting can bring to a classroom situation. Since the site was constructed both by the instructor and by his students, it demonstrates the ways that Web sites are often collaborative projects with multiple authors. The site also brings together course materials like the syllabus and policy statement, a collection of electronic texts used in the course, a series of student projects analyzing various texts, links to other related material not produced at the University of Texas, and a set of interactive comment forms that allow users to give feedback about the site. Because these features were all incorporated into a single collection of documents, the site truly evolved into the focal text for the course (both as a resource and as a site of production). Many of the questions on the midterm and final exams, in fact, came from the material produced on the Web site.

Nick Evans' American Literature Site.
Gloria McMillan's Hypertext Classics page
the American Studies web,
a collection of literary research tools on the web
a collection of arts and humanities gopher sites,
the library of congress home page,
the UT Libraries books online,
the cmu list of online book titles,
the El Net Galaxy's poetry page,

If you're interested in specific information for students,
see

the policy statement,
the reading schedule,
the first paper assignment,
the second paper assignment.

Return to Daniel's home page or the CWRL.

A short list of related resources and class materials

The site is organized along two basic axes: the four units of the class and the individual texts surveyed in the course. Each of the four course units—"American Stories," "America Shown *Real*," "American Poetry," and "American Scenes"—has a node that was linked from an imagemap on the home page.

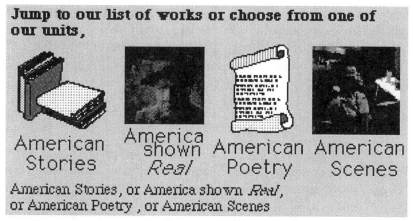

Jump to our list of works or choose from one of our units,

American Stories   America shown *Real*   American Poetry   American Scenes

American Stories, or America shown *Real*, or American Poetry , or American Scenes

An image map linking the four course units

The unit nodes are arranged around issues of theme, genre and/or period, and include electronic copies of the primary texts as well as student annotation, analysis and discussion.

American Stories

Our first unit familiarizes us with various American cultural themes and modes of reading early American texts. It is titled

American Stories.

Most of the texts for this unit are online and have been annotated with student comments or linked to sites containing transcripts of student discussions or compilations of student analyses. This unit contains...

a Rip Van Winkle site.
    This site contains the online text and links to student analyses.
a Legend of Sleepy Hollow site.

Index page of the "American Stories" unit

165

From the home page, the user also has the option of connecting to separate nodes organized around the class texts. These are the same pages that are available from within the larger unit nodes, but the instructor chose to duplicate their display by listing them individually. Thus, a user has the option of thinking about texts in connection with a particular unit of the course, or of accessing information about any one of the texts on its own.

Within each of the smaller, single text nodes the instructor and the students have compiled a significant amount of material about the literary work. For example, the pages which explore Charlotte Perkins Gilman's story "The Yellow Wall-Paper" provide an excellent illustration of the kinds of resources that a class can build using HTML. The site contains a number of links: the text of "The Yellow Wall-Paper"; another piece by Gilman entitled "Why I Wrote 'The Yellow Wall-Paper'"; an excerpt from Gilman's editor, H.E. Scudder, about

A small portion of the Yellow Wall-Paper Site

receiving the story; the class newsgroup; an HTML discussion forum; student essays about the story; a transcript of a real-time class discussion; *The Charlotte Perkins Gilman Newsletter*; another class site covering "The Yellow Wall-Paper"; and a discussion of a film version of the story. With this array of material, the site becomes a useful resource not only for this particular class, but also for other American literature classes that might be studying Gilman. And because of the interactive nature of the pages, the site will continue to grow as new visitors utilize the resource and offer feedback and commentary.

The instructor feels that perhaps the most interesting and productive aspect of the site has been the quantity and quality of feedback that he has received via comment forms. In fact, an in-depth analysis of this feedback could easily serve as a case study of its own. What we want to point out here is that the site, and especially "The Yellow Wall-Paper" node, has received a variety of different types of responses including: suggestions about better layout, commentary and questions about the story, film, site and the instructor's pedagogical practice, notes from the publishers of the film used by the class, notes from the publishers of *The Charlotte Perkins Gilman Newsletter*, requests from other college instructors to visit the site with their classes, contacts about including the site as part of an American Studies grant, and several comments from students who found the site helpful for their studies. The site was much more than an isolated, local space where students were required to post their essays. The pages were frequently visited by Web users who represented a diverse audience, and the feedback proved to be productive for both the instructor and the students.

What makes these outside connections so satisfying to the instructor is the fact that, while he organized the basic structure of the index pages, it was the students themselves who provided the lion's share of textual analysis. Students were introduced to the Web early in the term, and throughout the semester they worked alone and in groups to produce a variety of projects that appear on the site. Beginning with simple, text-only projects, students acquainted themselves with the basics of HTML scripting. Gradually, as they began to feel more comfortable with the medium, students learned how to incorporate graphics, imagemaps, sound and video clips into their projects.

In addition, students began thinking about stylistic and compositional issues: for example, they were forced to consider how sound or video clips can be implemented in an argument. Two student projects from the node exploring the play A *Raisin in the Sun* by Lorraine Hansberry illustrate this point.

In the first example, the student, perhaps trying to break up the text into manageable sections, offers this page design for her analysis of the play:

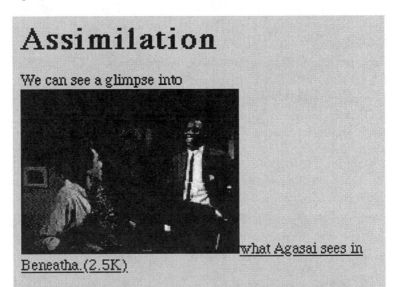

Index page for a student project on A Raisin in the Sun

This is actually a well-organized index page. The student has structured her information nicely and provided clear links to other pages. The problem, however, is that although it conforms adequately to the conventions of an index page on the Web, it is much less effective as a literary analysis about a scene in *A Raisin in the Sun*. Notice that the student has scripted her HTML document in a way that separates rather than combines the various media involved. A user is able to link to a short video clip, the corresponding text from the play, or the student's analysis of the scene; following any one of these

To be or not to be.....
African or American

In this scene we can see the apparent struggle that Beneatha makes in her soceity.... whether to fit in as an American, which would mean giving up her heritage, or reclaiming her ancestral roots. Asagai points out aspects of herself that she did not realize before. The comment about her hair being "mutilated" really hits home as she begans to look at her assimilatist ways. Beneatha appears to be a strong independant woman up until this point. Before when she makes the comment about possibly not getting married, one is to believe she can stand alone. But her sense of need to please Asagai and be more like him shows women to be "inadequate" without a man, and that they are constantly wondering what the men think of them. I think Asagai's comment is a bit contradictory. He makes the statement as if people who reclaim their ancestrial roots and ignore the society's set norms, then they will no longer be assimilatist. It appears to me that anyone trying to follow a certain way of life that other people live, are in essence assimilatists as well.

Return to the African Culture page, this project's homepage or The Rasin in the Sun's homepage.

Film analysis divorced from graphics and video

links, however, takes a reader away from this central organization and separates each of these texts from the others. The student's analysis of assimilationist thought in one particular scene of the play, for example, is displayed without either the still, the video, or the passage from the play.

The student makes some interesting points about assimilation and gender roles, but because of her organizational choices, a reader has to leave this page and link back to the index in order to see the video clip or read the text from the play. So although the student has used the Web to include a number of documents and media within her project, some of her design choices have lessened the rhetorical effectiveness of her argument.

A second student project about the same text does a better job of integrating the graphics and video into the flow of her argument.

But, as the time draws near for Walter to put his pride away he realizes with the help of the family that no amount of money can make up for the loss of pride and that it is sometimes better to sacrifice the goals of one for the good of many, so he tells the gentleman from the 'Welcoming Committee' that they "decided to move into our house because my father-my father-he earned it."

(To see supporting film footage and analysis, click above)
This bold and unselfish move helps to propagate the family's long standing ethics, values, and pride.

Graphics and video incorporated into a student argument

This student's incorporation of multimedia is much more seamless. She uses the graphics and video almost like a quotation from a book, describing and analyzing the scene in a way which makes clear exactly how she is reading this section of the film version. The strategy seems to be more effective than the earlier example in terms of the project's argument, yet we should note that overall, the second project is less structured than the first, and the student doesn't use the hypertextual linking capabilities of the Web to provide external links (for example, to the text of the play for a comparison).

Ultimately, what these examples point out is that composition on the Web is still in its early stages. Theories about the hypertextual nature of argument on the Web have come a long way since the first edition of this text was published, but are still in development. Tackling these difficult compositional issues will certainly pose some problems for instructors, but will also provide opportunities to begin charting the various rhetorical strategies that go into new forms of composition. By talking as a class about "what works" and "what doesn't work" in a project, and by discussing what causes those successes or failures, instructors can utilize the difficulties inherent in Web building to address effectively issues like style, audience, and organization.

Chapter Six: HTML and Web Composition

APPENDICES

Appendix One:
Additional Resources

Suggested Readings

Aoki, Kumiko. *Intercultural Telecollaboration: A Field Experiment Based upon a Heuristic Telecollaboration Model for Collaborative Writing Through the Internet.* Diss. U of Hawaii, 1995.

Anderson, Daniel. "From Browsers to Builders: Student Composition on the World Wide Web." *http://auden.en.utexas.edu/~daniel/browserstobuilders/* (30 April 1997).

___. "Not Maimed but Malted: Nodes, Text and Graphics in Freshmen Compositions." *CWRL, The Electronic Journal for Computer Writing, Rhetoric and Literature. http://www.en.utexas.edu/~cwrl/v1n1/article1/notmaimedbutmalted.html* (30 April 1997).

___, Bret Benjamin, and Bill Paredes-Holt. *Connections: A Guide to On-Line Writing.* NY: Allyn & Bacon, 1997.

Barrett, Edward, ed. *The Society of Text: Hypertext, Hypermedia, and the Social Construction of Information.* Technical Communication and Information Systems. Cambridge and London: MIT, 1989.

Bauman, Marcy. "Negotiating a Passage Among Readers and Writers on the Web." *Computer-Mediated Communication Magazine* 4.6 (1997). *http://www.december.com/cmc/mag/1997/jun/bauman.html* (15 July 1997).

Bennahum, David. "Fly Me to the MOO: Adventures in Textual Reality." *Lingua Franca.* May/June, 1994: 1, 22-36.

Berge, Zane L., and Mauri P. Collins, eds. *Computer Mediated Communication and the Online Classroom.* Cresskill, NJ: Hampton Press, 1995. 3 vols.

Berk, Emily, and Joe Devlin, eds. *Hypertext/Hypermedia Handbook.* New York: McGraw-Hill, 1991.

Bolter, Jay David. *Writing Space: The Computer, Hypertext, and the History of Writing.* Hillsdale, NJ: Lawrence Erlbaum, 1991.

Bruce, Bertram, Joy Kreeft Peyton, and Trent Batson, eds. *Networked-Based Classrooms: Promises and Realities* Cambridge: Cambridge UP, 1993.

Bruckman, Amy. "Gender Swapping On The Internet." *ftp:// ftp.media.mit.edu pub/asb/papers/gender-swapping.txt* (30 April 1997).

Bruffee, K., Kathleen Blair, Marylyn Cooper and Cynthia L. Selfe. "Two Comments on Computer Conferences and Learning: Authority, Resistance, and Internally Persuasive Discourse." *College English* 53 (1991): 55-95.

Chernaik, Warren, Caroline Davis, and Marilyn Deegan, eds. *The Politics of the Electronic Text.* Oxford: Office for Humanities Communication, 1993.

Cherny, Lynn, and Elizabeth Rose Weise, eds. *Wired Women: Gender and New Realities in Cyberspace.* Seattle: Seal Press, 1996.

Cooper, Marylyn M, and Cynthia L. Selfe. "Computer Conferences and Learning: Authority, Resistance, and Internally Persuasive Discourse." *College English* 52 (1990): 847-869.

Daisley, Margaret. "The Game of Literacy: The Meaning of *Play* in Computer-Mediated Communication." *Computers and Composition* 11 (1994) 107-119.

December, John. "The Myths and Realities of World Wide Web Publishing." *Computer-Mediated Communication Magazine* 4.5 (1997). *http://www.december.com/cmc/mag/1997/may/december.html* (15 July 1997).

Delany, Paul. "The Discourse of Computer-Supported Media: Reading and Writing on Usenet." *Yearbook of English Studies* 25 (1995): 213-24.

Dery, Mark, ed. *Flame Wars: The Discourse of Cyberculture.* Durham, NC: Duke UP, 1994.

Faigley, L. "Subverting the Electronic Workbook: Teaching Writing Using Networked Computers." *Writing Teacher as Researcher: Essays in the Theory and Practice of Class-Based Research.* Eds. Donald A. Daker and Max Morenberg. Portsmouth NH: Boynton/Cook, 1990: 290-311.

Glaros, Michelle. "Playing in the MUDs." *Play.* April, 1994: 52-55.

Hawisher, Gail, and Cynthia Selfe. "The Rhetoric of Technology and the Electronic Writing Class." *College Composition and Communication* 42 (1991): 55-65.

___, and Charles Moran. "Electronic Mail and the Writing Instructor." *College English* 55 (1993): 627-643.

Herring, Susan C., ed. *Computer-Mediated Communication: Linguistic, Social and Cross-Cultural Perspectives.* Amsterdam: Benjamins, 1996.

Johnson-Eilola, Johndan. "Control and the Cyborg: Writing and Being Written in Hypertext." *Journal of Advanced Composition* 13 (1993): 381-400.

Kaplan, Nancy. "Politexts, Hypertexts, and Other Cultural Formations in the Late Age of Print." *Computer-Mediated Communica-*

tion 2.3 (1995). *http://sunsite.unc.edu/cmc/mag/1995/mar/ kaplan.html* (30 April 1997).

Kemp, F. "The User-Friendly Fallacy." *College Composition and Communication* 38 (1987): 32-39.

___. "Getting Smart with Computers: Computer Aided Heuristics for Student Writers." *Writing Center Journal* 8.1 (1987): 32-39.

Landow, George P. *Hypertext: The Convergence of Contemporary Critical Theory and Technology.* Baltimore: Johns Hopkins UP, 1992.

___, and Paul Delany, eds. *The Digital Word: Text-Based Computing in the Humanities.* Cambridge: MIT Press, 1993.

Lanham, Richard. *The Electronic Word: Democracy, Technology, and the Arts.* Chicago: U of Chicago P, 1993.

Laurel, Brenda. *Computers as Theatre.* Reading, MA: Addison-Wesley, 1991.

Madden, Ed. "Women, Gods, and Monsters: Using Hypertexts in the Literature Classroom." *CWRL, The Electronic Journal for Computer Writing, Rhetoric and Literature. http://www.en.utexas.edu/ ~cwrl/v1n2/article3/madden.html* (30 April 1997).

McGann, Jerome. "The Rationale of Hypertext." *http:// www.village.virginia.edu/public/jjm2f/rationale.html* (15 July 1997).

McKnight, C., A. Dillon, and J. Richardson, eds. *Hypertext: A Psychological Perspective.* Hornwood Series in Interactive Communication Systems. New York and London: Ellis Hornwood, 1993.

Moulthrop, Stuart. "Traveling in the Breakdown Lane: A Principle of Resistance for Hypertext." *http://www.ubalt.edu/www/ygcla/sam/essays/breakdown.html* (28 July 1997).

___, "The Shadow of an Informand: An Experiment in Hypertext Rhetoric." *http://raven.ubalt.edu/staff/moulthrop/hypertexts/* (28 July 1997).

Nelson, Theodor Holm. *Literary Machines.* San Antonio: n.p., 1987.

Owen, Trevor, Ron Owston, and Cheryl Dickie, eds. *The Learning Highway: A Student's Guide to the Internet.* Toronto: Key Porter Books, 1995.

Papert, Seymour. *The Children's Machine: Rethinking School in the Age of the Computer.* New York: Basic Books, 1993.

Postman, Neil. "Teaching as an Amusing Activity." *Amusing Ourselves to Death: Public Discourse in the Age of Show Business.* New York: Penguin, 1985: 143-154.

Quinn, Carolyn Knox. "Authentic Classroom Experiences: Anonymity, Mystery and Improvisation in Synchronous Writing Environments." *CWRL, The Electronic Journal for Computer Writing, Rhetoric and Literature.* *http://www.en.utexas.edu/~cwrl/v1n2/article2/aspect1.html* (30 April 1997).

Quittner, Josh. "The War Between alt.tasteless and rec.pets.cats." *Wired.* May, 1994: 46-52.

Regan, Allison. "'Type Normal Like the Rest of Us': Writing, Power, and Homophobia in the Networked Composition Classroom." *Computers and Composition* 10 (1993): 11-23.

Romano, Susan. "The Egalitarian Narrative: Whose Story? Which Yardstick?" *Computers and Composition* 10 (1993): 25-28.

Rowlett, Douglas. "Plucking the Spider's Web: Why I Use High Technology and the Internet in the Classroom." *Southwestern Studies* 3.1 (1995): 11-17.

Selfe, Cynthia L. "Computer-Based Conversations and the Changing Nature of Collaboration." *New Visions of Collaborative Writing*. Ed. Janis Forman. Portsmouth, NH: Boynton/Cook, 1992. 147-169.

___, and Susan Hilligoss, eds. *Literacy and Computers: The Complications of Teaching and Learning with Technology*. Modern Language Association Series on Research and Scholarship in Composition. New York: Modern Language Association, 1994.

Slatin, John. "Hypertext and the Teaching of Writing." *Text, conText, and hyperText: Writing with and for the Computer*. Ed. E. Barrett. Cambridge: MIT Press, 1988. 111-129.

___. "Is There a Class in this Text? Creating Knowledge in the Electronic Classroom." *Sociomedia: Multimedia, Hypermedia, and the Social Construction of Knowledge*. Ed. E. Barrett. Cambridge: MIT Press, 1992. 28-52.

Stephenson, Neal. "Smiley's People." *New Republic* 13 Sept. 1993: 26.

Sutter, J. Ramsey. "Caught in the Web: The Internet, Education, Technology, and the Myth of Higher Learning." *Southwestern Studies* 3.1 (1995): 1-10.

Sutton, Laurel. "Using Usenet: Gender, Power, and Silence in Electronic Discourse." *Proceedings of the Twentieth Annual Meeting of the Berkeley Linguistics Society*. Berkeley: Berkeley Linguistics Society, 1994. 506-20.

Syverson, M. A. *The Wealth of Reality: An Ecology of Composition.* Diss. U of California, San Diego, 1994.

Tuman, Myron C., ed. *Literacy Online: The Promise (and Peril) of Writing with Computers.* Pittsburgh and London: Pittsburgh UP, 1992.

Warshauer, Susan. "Aesthetic Approaches to the Design and Study of MUDs (Multi-User Domains) in English and Performance Studies: Interface, Realism and the Dialectic of Interacting." *CWRL, The Electronic Journal for Computer Writing, Rhetoric and Literature.* *http://www.en.utexas.edu/~cwrl/v1n1/article3/mudmain.html* (30 April 1997).

Wiener, Jon. "Free Speech on the Internet." *The Nation* 13 June, 1994: 825-828.

Wright, Robert. "Voice of America." *New Republic* 13 Sept. 1993: 20+.

Useful Sites and Addresses

INTERNET PEDAGOGY

Computer Writing and Research Lab
http://www.en.utexas.edu/

The Computer-Mediated Communications Study Center
http://www.december.com/cmc/study/center.html

Constructivist Project Design Guide. Includes pedagogical rationale (mostly K-12) as well as hands-on advice about Web page building.
http://www.ilt.columbia.edu/k12/livetext-nf/webcurr.html

E-MAIL

- GENERAL INFORMATION
  http://www.cis.ohio-state.edu/hypertext/faq/usenet/mail/top.html

- LISTSERV INFORMATION
  http://www.tile.net/tile/listserv/index.html

International E-mail Classroom Connections List. To subscribe send a message containing the word "subscribe" to *iecc-request@stolaf.edu*

NEWSGROUPS

- GENERAL INFORMATION
  http://www.cis.ohio-state.edu/hypertext/faq/usenet/FAQ-List.html

  http://www.tile.net/tile/news/index.html

MU*S

- GENERAL INFORMATION
  ftp://media.mit.edu/pub/MediaMOO/

  http://www.clock.org/muds/

- MU* ADDRESSES
  MIT's Media MOO. Geared more toward researchers than students. *Telnet://purple-crayon.media.mit.edu:8888*

  DU (Diversity University). A MOO designed for students and classes. You can use these facilities to interact or to build spaces for class use. *Telnet://moo.du.org:8888*

  Daedalus MOO. Designed to promote discussion of issues related to Daedalus computer and composition software and to provide a less structured space for teachers to bring their students. *Telnet://logos.daedalus.com:7777*

  Virtual Online University (VOU) Geared toward exploring and facilitating distance education. *Telnet://athena.edu 8888* or access their WWW home page at *http://www.athena.edu/*

  PMC MOO. Sponsored by the online magazine *Postmodern Culture*, this MOO provides a space for researchers to come and talk about theory and practice. *Telnet://hero.village.virginia.edu:7777*

HTML

- GENERAL INFORMATION
  The UT Austin Learning Web
  http://www.utexas.edu/learn/pub/

HTML Information at Toronto
http://www.utoronto.ca/webdocs/HTMLdocs/NewHTML/
htmlindex.html

The Yahoo Web and HTML Site
http://www.yahoo.com/Computers_and_Internet/
Software/Data_Formats/HTML/

- PEDAGOGY AND STYLE
  Kairos: A Journal for Teachers of Writing in Webbed
  Environments.
  http://english.ttu.edu/kairos/index.html

  Yale C/AIM WWW Style Manual
  http://info.med.yale.edu/caim/manual/

  Style Guide for Online Hypertext
  http://www.w3.org/pub/WWW/Style/Overview.html

  CWRL information on HTML in the classroom
  http://www.en.utexas.edu/instructors/introducinghtml/
  introducinghtml.html

Appendix Two:
Copyright Issues

Instructors increasingly have to work with copyright considerations as they prepare their course material. The "fair use clause" of the US Copyright Act gives instructors some flexibility when it comes to using copyrighted materials in the classroom:

> Not withstanding the provisions of sections 106 and 106A [17 USCS §§ 106, 106A] the fair use of a copyrighted work, including such use by reproduction in copies or phonorecords or by any other means specified by that section, for purposes such as criticism, comment, news reporting, teaching (including multiple copies for classroom use), scholarship, or research, is not an infringement of copyright. In determining whether the use made of a work in any particular case is a fair use the factors to be considered shall include—
>
> (1) the purpose and character of the use, including whether such use is of a commercial nature or is for nonprofit educational purposes;
> (2) the nature of the copyrighted work;
> (3) the amount and substantiality of the portion used in relation to the copyrighted work as a whole; and
> (4) the effect of the use upon the potential market for or value of the copyrighted work.
>
> The fact that a work is unpublished shall not itself bar a finding of fair use if such finding is made upon consideration of all the above factors.

Under these guidelines, it is possible to make use of copyrighted materials for the purpose of instruction. However, the inter-connectedness and spontaneous nature of the net complicates the notion of what constitutes the fair use of copyrighted materials. For example, duplicating an essay or an ad from a magazine for use in class might fall under the guidelines for fair use of copyrighted material because it is done for scholarly or critical purposes and not intended to make a profit. Posting the same material to a class newsgroup, however, might not be acceptable because it would be available to an audience outside the classroom and this availability might diminish the value of the original document. Perhaps even sending the article as an e-mail message would have the same effect, since e-mail messages are often forwarded to secondary parties. Posting materials on the World Wide Web compounds the problem of fair use because most Web browsers allow users to download any materials they find and to incorporate the source documents of Web pages into their own sites.

Because of the simplicity of distributing materials on the net, making clear distinctions about the boundaries of copyrighted materials becomes difficult. The rights of intellectual property owners should be balanced with those of individuals who wish to participate in the free exchange of ideas. In their statement, "Fair Use in the Electronic Age: Serving the Public Interest," the American Library Association suggests that the balance between the owner's claims to intellectual property and the public's interest in the free exchange of ideas should be honored in electronic space.

> The primary objective of copyright is not to reward the labor of authors, but "[t]o promote the Progress of Science and useful Arts." To this end, copyright assures authors the right to their original expression, but encourages others to build freely upon the ideas and information conveyed by a work....This result is neither unfair nor unfortunate. It is the means by which copyright advances the progress of science and art. — Justice Sandra Day O'Connor (Feist Publications, Inc. v. Rural Telephone Service Co., 499 US 340, 349 (1991) The genius of United

States copyright law is that, in conformance with its constitutional foundation, it balances the intellectual property interests of authors, publishers and copyright owners with society's need for the free exchange of ideas.

The guidelines of the fair use clause can be applied to the Internet as well, but instructors should be aware that many of the issues relating to electronic use of material, and particularly electronic scholarly use, are still unresolved. Some guidelines include using no more materials than necessary to make a given point, and considering whether using certain materials will devalue them in any way for the owner.

You will also find some material already online which probably shouldn't be, for example scanned pictures, unauthorized reproductions of texts, film clips, and sound files. When evaluating sources, you and your students should strive to comply with fair use guidelines by considering the implications of using materials which are available online but which may not be in the public domain.

A related concern is the impact of posting material online, especially student papers and other texts. We advise having students sign waivers which state that the texts they produce in classes will be considered public discourse. There are no mechanisms in place on the Internet for assuring that the papers posted by students won't at some point be downloaded and made use of in less than responsible ways. Instructors will have to heighten our awareness of these considerations when placing materials on the net.

Appendix Two: Copyright Issues

Appendix Three:
Online Citation Formats

Major documentation systems like the APA and the MLA have recently incorporated guidelines for citing Internet sources in their style guides; however, because they duplicate the format of traditional documentation forms without accommodating the particular demands of the Internet, we think their suggestions fail to provide the necessary citation information for Internet resources.

The MLA Handbook offers the following guide for Internet sources.

Material accessed through a computer network

1 Name of the author (if given)
2. Title of the article or document (in quotation marks)
3. Title of the journal, newsletter or conference (underlined)
4. Volume number, issue number or other identifying number
5. Year or date of publication (in parentheses)
6. Number of pages or paragraphs (if given) or *n.pag* ("no pagination")
7. Publication medium (*Online*)
8. Name of the computer network
9. Date of access

A sample entry would look like this:

Moulthrop, Stuart. "You Say You Want a Revolution? Hypertext and the Laws of Media." <u>Postmodern</u>

<u>Culture</u> 1.3 (1991) : 53 pars. Online. BITNET. 10 Jan.
1993

According to the MLA, at the end of the entry you may add as
supplementary information the electronic address you used to access
the document; precede the address with the word "Available." They
note that "[y]our instructor may require this information."

Though it is a convention that tries to indicate the existence of
Internet sources, this system does little to handle the unique nature
of Internet publications. Simply telling a reader that a source can be
found "online" does little to help a researcher find the source document. It would be very difficult to locate this source again and to
determine if you had the same version of the document. Because of
the Internet's vast scope and changing nature, it is especially important to provide the exact path by which you found a document and
to distinguish between the date you found the source and its publication date (if it has one).

You may want to discuss these problems of citation and issues of
conventions with your students, and you will need to have a useful
citation guide so that you can find Internet sources. The location of
resources will likely include an Internet protocol, an address and a
path (for example, *ftp://ftp.media.mit.edu/pub/asb/papers/*). While you
may want to develop your own style guide to handle the subtle distinctions in Internet media, we would like to suggest using an existing style sheet that adapts the MLA guidelines to the particularities
of Internet sources very well.

Janice R. Walker of the Department of English at the University of
South Florida has developed a style guide for handling Internet resources that distinguishes between different protocols and highlights
the importance of addresses in each. The components of her reference citation are simply:

Author's Lastname, Author's Firstname. "Title of Document." *Title of Complete Work* (if applicable). Version or File Number, if applicable. Document date or date of last revision (if different from access date). Protocol and address, access path or directories (date of access).

For example, a citation for a resource located on the Web would look like this:

Bruckman, Amy. "Approaches to Managing Deviant Behavior in Virtual Communities." Apr. 1994. ftp:// ftp.media.mit.edu/pub/asb/papers/deviance-chi94 (4 Dec. 1994).

Walker has placed a style sheet on the Web that provides a documentation system for all the different Internet media we cover in this book. Endorsed by the Alliance for Computers & Writing and other organizations, the style sheet is located at *http://www.cas.usf.edu/ english/walker/mla.html.* We would recommend introducing your students to Walker's guide as an addition to the MLA handbook for citing Internet sources. (For a more complete discussion of citation formats, see the *Columbia Guide to Online Style* by Janice R. Walker and Todd Taylor, Columbia University Press.)

Appendix Three: Online Citation Formats

Appendix Four:
Telnet and FTP

Telnet

Telnet is a terminal emulation protocol: with a Telnet client, you can establish a connection to a remote computer, almost like being at that machine's keyboard. Once connected, a user can work with files in a specific portion of the computer's operating system (a "shell"), access files being shared by a server program, or activate other client programs that reside on the remote machine. Note that in common usage, the term "Telnet" both describes the process of making internet connections, and denotes the name of client applications which perform this function, such as NCSA Telnet and Trumpet Telnet.

A Telnet connection is the most basic of all Internet functions. Before media like Gopher and the Web were available, researchers often used Telnet applications to connect directly to a site which offered a specific kind of database. An example of such a site is *info.umd.edu* at the University of Maryland. It offers an electronic archive of government documents (from the text of legislative bills to transcripts of presidential press conferences), and is thus an excellent resource. While you might still use a Telnet application to connect directly to such sites, more and more such archives are making their text files available through the World Wide Web (and some, increasingly, exclusively so).

While some of the Internet functions will vary, a user has two basic options for using a Telnet client to access information on the net. For example, when reading e-mail a user could:

- Telnet to a shell on a mainframe and log on to the machine's mailserver in order to read text files directly from the server.
- Telnet to a shell on a mainframe and activate a mail reading client that resides on that machine. This remote client program will offer the reader an improved interface for managing mail. Note, however, that this interface is still limited by the simplicity of the Telnet connection.

If you use other workstation client software, you will probably not make extensive use of Telnet applications, or make direct Telnet connections yourself.

NCSA Telnet and Trumpet Telnet are freeware applications which you can download from a variety of sites, or obtain directly from your institution. As we recommend so often in this book, speak with your systems administrator if you have any questions about how you will be using Telnet at your institution.

File Transfer Protocol (FTP)

FTP is a basic means by which files—including text files, graphics, even applications themselves—are downloaded from and uploaded to central sites by users working at their desktop computers. Because FTP client programs can be used to download Internet software, they should be one of the first applications you obtain (probably from your computation center). Transferring files can be a difficult process (though made easier by client programs), and we do not have the opportunity here to explain it fully. Some of the issues you will need to be concerned with are: knowing the address of a site which contains the materials you want, negotiating the directory structure on that site, choosing the right settings for downloading the files, and decompressing these files to produce the resources you desire. Your institution may maintain its own FTP site with appropriate software for your system.

FTP Sites With Internet Client Software:

ftp.utexas.edu (Mac only)
dartvax.dartmouth.edu
wuarchive.wustl.edu
ftp.ncsa.uiuc.edu
sumex-aim.stanford.edu

Although file transfers can be performed with programs resident on institutional servers (often by typing "ftp" and an address at the prompt), we strongly recommend that you look into client software for this procedure—it will alleviate many of the difficulties involved in transferring files. Most of these applications also allow you to save site addresses, login names, and directory paths as bookmarks, so you can return to especially useful sites with one click of the mouse.

Because files on FTP sites are sometimes compressed in a variety of different formats, you will probably need to have on hand several different applications for decompression. The format used for decompression will be indicated by the filename's suffix (for example: .sit, .tar, .zip). The best kind of files to come across (if you don't have client software) are self-extracting archives (.sea), which require no decompression software; unfortunately, however, a lot of material is not compressed using this method. Decompression software is available around the Internet for downloading, but tends to be shareware rather than freeware. You will have to balance your needs for downloading with how many licensing fees your budget can afford. Speak with your systems administrator about the decompression software you might need for particular files, as well as how to obtain and configure client software for FTP.

You may also use FTP for uploading files to a server, most likely to publish World Wide Web documents. When loading files, make sure that HTML documents and any text files are sent as "ASCII text" or "text only" and that other media are transported as "binary" or "raw data." Also make sure that file names remain unaltered during the uploading process. (To do so, deselect settings on the FTP client application which append extensions to the file names.)

Appendix Five:
Client/Server Interaction

Although it is common to think of an Internet server as an actual computer, in reality servers are programs which reside on network-connected machines. What distinguishes a server program from other software is that it provides files and information for use by client programs. These clients are a separate set of applications that "talk" to servers and access the data they offer. Internet media are distinguished by the types of protocols they use, each protocol a "language" allowing Internet clients and servers to communicate. For example, a mail reading client would access a mail server using the shared language of SMTP (Simple Mail Transfer Protocol) or, similarly, an FTP client and server interact using File Transfer Protocol.

All of the Internet applications we discuss require that your local machine have some sort of connection with an Internet server. While you may not need to learn Unix commands and the intricacies of server operations, we do recommend that you learn to work closely with your systems administrator in order to take full advantage of the Internet possibilities we cover. In order to set up a class listserv, newsgroup, MU* space, or Web site, you will need to negotiate any number of server operations, first with the assistance of a systems administrator and then based on your own knowledge and ability.

While some of the Internet functions will vary, a user has three basic options for accessing information on the net. For example, when reading e-mail a user could:

- telnet to a shell on a mainframe and log on to the machine's mail server.

- telnet to a shell on a mainframe and activate a mail reading client that resides on that machine.
- operate a mail reading client located on her own personal computer. Throughout the book we refer to these programs as "workstation clients."

Although very basic, Telnet is among the most versatile of Internet clients in that it can communicate with servers using a number of different protocols. Thus, Telnet facilitates a wide range of activities with a very simple computer system. You can connect to Telnet servers (like library catalogs and other databases), MU* servers, or mail servers. However, a Telnet connection to a remote server does not provide an intuitive interface and often requires that you know a number of specialized commands. Additionally, Telnet connections offer very few features for archiving your interactions.

Client programs which can be operated through a Telnet connection provide a user with greater flexibility than the Telnet connection alone. Through Telnet, you can log on to an account on an Internet-connected computer and activate various client programs which reside there. For example, a user could connect to remote mail and news reading clients and use their easier interface to read, compose and store messages. In addition, users often access remote clients to navigate MU*s much more efficiently. Many accounts also provide a Gopher client, and some provide limited access to the World Wide Web using Lynx, a text-only Web browser. While all of these remote client programs offer greater utility than a direct Telnet connection to a server, they are still less "friendly" than workstation client software.

If at all possible, you should use workstation client software. These are programs that operate on your personal computer and control your interface with Internet servers. The limitation of using this type of client software is that these programs often require a faster Internet connection (especially for newsreaders and graphical Web browsers) and a more powerful personal computer. In return, however, workstation client software offers an easy interface that lets you concentrate less on the technology and more on teaching. Besides making Internet operations almost transparent, workstation client software offers the best features for viewing, retrieving, saving, storing, and composing. The client programs themselves are simple to install and readily available as freeware and shareware.

FTP Sites With Client Software:

ftp.utexas.edu (mac only)
dartvax.dartmouth.edu
wuarchive.wustl.edu
ftp.ncsa.uiuc.edu
sumex-aim.stanford.edu

A Few Workstation Client Programs

	Mac	**Windows**
Telnet	NCSA Telnet	Trumpet Telnet
FTP client	Fetch	WS_FTP
Mail readers	Eudora	Weudora
Newsreaders	Newswatcher Nuntius	WinVN Trumpet News
MU* clients	MUDDweller Mudling	MUTT MudWin
IRC clients	IRCle	MIRC

Gopher browsers	Turbogopher	WSgopher
WWW browsers	Netscape	Netscape
	Internet Explorer	Internet Explorer

Remember, this book was revised in 1997 and these applications and their operations are likely to change. Mosaic, the first graphical Web browser, was introduced in the fall of 1993. Netscape followed in the spring of 1994, adopted by 75% of all Web users by the end of that year. As of 1997, Netscape retains approximately the same proportionate share of a much larger market, with Microsoft's Internet Explorer making up much of the difference.

Appendix Six:
Additional MOO Commands

Below are some of the basic commands used to create rooms, exits and objects in a MOO. Because of the growing tendency for the more "academically oriented" of MU* spaces to be constructed using MOO scripts, we provide these MOO commands. Those details which do apply specifically to MOOs, however, can almost always be adapted with only minor variations to the other MU* formats.

Each of these commands should be followed by the name of the component you wish to change, and/or a text description. This list is by no means exhaustive or descriptive; it is simply intended as a means to get you started. Consulting the online help will be the best way to get a complete listing of the building commands available on any particular MOO. For help with a command once online, simply type "help" and then the command name.

@dig "[new-room-name]"
    creates a room

@desc [object] as "[description]"
    describes a room or an object

@add-exit
    creates an exit

@add-entrance
    creates an entrance

@dig [direction] to "[room]"
    links an exit and an entrance

@leave
> defines what you see just before you go through an exit

@oleave
> what others see when you leave

@arrive
> what you see after you arrive in a room

@oarrive
> what others see when you arrive in a room

@lock
> prevents other users from entering rooms or taking an object

@nogo
> what you see if you can't go through an exit

@onogo
> what others see if you can't go through an exit

@create [object type] named "[name]"
> creates a new object of a given type ($note, $letter, $thing, or $container)

@take
> picks up an object

@take_succeeded
> what you see when you take

@otake_succeeded
> what others see when you take

@take_failed
> what you see if you can't take

@otake_failed
> what others see if you can't take

@drop
> drops an object

@drop_succeeded
> what you see when you drop

@odrop_succeeded
> what others see when you drop

@drop_failed
> what you see when you can't drop

@odrop_failed
> what others see when you can't drop

Appendix Six: MOO Commands

Appendix Seven:
Additional HTML Information

HTML Commands

HTML instructions, together with the text to which the instructions apply, are called HTML elements. The HTML instructions are in turn called tags, and are comprised of the element name surrounded by left and right angle brackets. For example, all Web pages begin with the element <HTML> so that Web browsers immediately identify the document as an HTML file.

Most elements mark blocks of the document text for purposes of formatting. The end of a formatted section is marked by an ending tag, with the leading slash character "/" in front of the element name: </HTML>.

Some elements are "empty"—that is, they do not affect a block of the document. These elements do not require an ending tag. For example, the single tag <HR> draws a horizontal line across the page.

HTML documents themselves are broken into two main sections, the head and the body. Each section begins with a tag designating the section, and closes with an ending tag:

```
<HEAD>  . . .  </HEAD>
<BODY>  . . .  </BODY>
```

The head portion specifies information that browsers and servers use to search and organize documents. The most important component of a document's head is the <TITLE> element, which provides the information that appears at the top of the browsing window and is used for most keyword searches:

```
<TITLE> . . . </TITLE>
```

Often, Java scripts are also placed in the document head, to manage information and perform complex functions (a message forum, for example). The majority of additional commands, however, will be incorporated into the body of the document.

Headings

Headings dictate the size of selected text in the body of an HTML document, and should not be confused with the <HEAD> element.

```
<H1> . . . </H1>—largest header
<H2> . . . </H2>
<H3> . . . </H3>
<H4> . . . </H4>
<H5> . . . </H5>
<H6> . . . </H6>—smallest header
```

The placement of the headings may also be dictated by adding to the heading element an ALIGN attribute, now supported by most Web browsers. The possible values for headings are ALIGN="left," ALIGN="center," or ALIGN="right." For example, the element

```
<H1 ALIGN="center"> . . . </H1>
```

will both give the text between the tags the largest heading size, and center that text on the page. Note the use of quotes within the tag itself. If no ALIGN attribute is included, the heading will default to left-side alignment.

Font Styles

```
<B> . . . </B> — Boldface text
<I> . . . </I> — Italicized text
<U> . . . </U> — Underlined text
<STRIKE> . . . </STRIKE> — Strikethru text
<TT> . . . </TT> — Typewriter font
<BIG> . . . </BIG> — Large font
<SMALL> . . . </SMALL> — Small font
<SUP> . . . </SUP> — Superscript text
<SUB> . . . </SUB> — Subscript text
<CENTER> . . . </CENTER> —      Centered material
```

Lists & Menus

Definition list—presents a list of items with definitions for each appearing on an indented line below:

```
<DL>
<DT> First term
<DD> Definition
<DT> Next term
<DD> Definition
</DL>
```

Unnumbered list—presents a list with bullets appearing before each item:

```
<UL>
<LI> First item in the list
<LI> Next item in the list
</UL>
```

Numbered list—presents a list with numbers appearing before each item:

```
<OL>
<LI> First item in the list
<LI> Next item in the list
</OL>
```

Menu—presents a list in which each item appears indented:

```
<MENU>
<LI> First item in the menu
<LI> Next item
</MENU>
```

Links

The most common is the link to a document or file:

```
<A HREF="URL/file name"> . . . </A>
```

You can also make a link to a target within a document. Begin by placing a target anchor at the desired spot in the document:

```
<A NAME="target name">
```

Next, make a link to the target by using the "#" sign and specifying the target name in the link information:

```
<A HREF="#target name"> . . . </A>
```

You can also link to a sound, graphic, or video file by specifying the proper file name in the link information:

```
<A HREF="URL/filename.gif"> . . . </A>
```
links to a gif image
```
<A HREF="URL/filename.jpg"> . . . </A>
```
links to a jpeg image

```
<A HREF="URL/filename.mpg"> . . . </A>
   links to an mpeg movie
<A HREF="URL/filename.mov"> . . . </A>
   links to a Quicktime movie
<A HREF="URL/filename.au"> . . . </A>
   links to a sound file
<A HREF="URL/filename.wav"> . . . </A>
   links to a sound file
```

Inline Images

Inline images are graphics which are incorporated into the layout of a Web page. To place an inline image in a document, select the point in the document where the image should appear and use the command

```
<IMG ALIGN="bottom" SRC="imagefilename.gif">
```

The ALIGN attribute ("bottom" in the example) controls where surrounding text will appear in relation to the graphic. The standard alignments are "top," "middle," and "bottom," as well as "left" and "right." With left and right alignment, the image is aligned with the selected margin, and the text following the <IMG> element in the HTML script flows around the image.

With any inline image, remember to include an ALT attribute in the element, which specifies an alternate textual description of the image (add ALT=". . ." to the string of attributes in the <IMG> tag). This feature is a courtesy to users with slower modem connections who have turned off automatic image loading on their Web browsers.

Background Feature

The BACKGROUND attribute allows the user to specify an image file to be "tiled" as a background for the Web page. This attribute is applied to the <BODY> element, discussed above. For example, at the beginning of the body section of a Web page, the element

```
<BODY BACKGROUND="imagename.gif">
```

tiles the window background with the designated GIF image. When the background feature is utilized, the end tag to the body section is still simply: </BODY>.

Colors

Since the first edition of this text was published, the use of color on Web pages has expanded widely, and is supported by most Web browsers. Colors can be given to a number of page elements. In HTML, colors are designated by six-character codes representing their relative red/green/blue (RGB) values. Because of the incredible complexity of these codes, we recommend you use an HTML editor which supports the application of color. In such an editor, a shade is selected from a color wheel and the corresponding RGB values are placed automatically in the HTML script. Also, you might refer to one of the many Web sites that provides the codes for the 256 most commonly-used shades (for example, *http://www.onr.com/user/lights/netcol.html*).

Colors are applied as attributes to the <BODY> element, and should be specified in the opening tag. If one of the following attributes is used, they should *all* be specified in order to avoid color conflicts (such as a visitor to your page having set their Web browser to display text in the same color you gave to your background).

```
<BODY BGCOLOR="#rrggbb">
```
    sets the background color for the page as a whole

```
<BODY TEXT="#rrggbb">
```
    sets the text color for the page as a whole

```
<BODY LINK="#rrggbb">
```
    sets the unvisited link color for the page as a whole

```
<BODY VLINK="#rrggbb">
```
    sets the visited link color for the page as a whole

```
<BODY ALINK="#rrggbb">
```
    sets the activated link color for the page as a whole

All these attributes should be specified in a single <BODY> tag, like so:

```
<BODY BGCOLOR="#rrggbb" TEXT="#rrggbb"
LINK="#rrggbb" VLINK="#rrggbb"
ALINK="#rrggbb">
```

Colors may also be applied to selected text within the body of a Web page. The element

```
<FONT COLOR="#rrggbb"> . . . </FONT>
```

will set the color of the text between the tags to the designated shade.

Tables

HTML tables are contained within <TABLE> . . . </TABLE> tags. The fundamental elements of an HTML table are <CAPTION>, which defines a caption for the table, and <TR>, which defines a table row. Each row in turn contains cells, either for a header, defined by <TH>, or for data, defined by <TD>. (Although in this example we are using only numerical data, text and even graphic files can be entered in a data cell as well.) Each cell should be closed with the appropriate ending tag, either </TH> or </TD>.

The caption may be aligned to the top, bottom, left, or right of the table by adding an ALIGN attribute to the <CAPTION> tag. As for the alignment of the table itself, by default it is flush with the left margin, but it can be centered by placing the entire table script within <CENTER> . . . </CENTER> tags. Additionally, a BORDER attribute may be added to the <TABLE> tag, which indicates that the table should be drawn with a border around it and between each of the table's cells. Adding a value (in number of pixels) sets the outer border of the table to the specified width.

Combining all these features, then, the following script:

```
<CENTER> <TABLE BORDER=10>
<CAPTION ALIGN="bottom">Table Caption</CAPTION>
<TR> <TH>Heading 1</TH> <TH>Heading 2</TH>
   <TH>Heading 3</TH> </TR>
<TR> <TD>0.8</TD> <TD>1.2</TD> <TD>4.6</TD> </TR>
<TR> <TD>5.4</TD> <TD>0.44</TD> <TD>3.7</TD> </TR>
<TR> <TD>2.5</TD> <TD>6.2</TD> <TD>3.5</TD> </TR>
</TABLE> </CENTER>
```

produces a table displayed as:

Heading 1	Heading 2	Heading 3
0.8	1.2	4.6
5.4	0.44	3.7
2.5	6.2	3.5
Table Caption		

You can also experiment with adding the CELLPADDING= and CELLSPACING= attributes to the <TABLE> element, which dictate (in number of pixels) the amount of space surrounding the contents of cells, and the width of the borders between cells, respectively. More complex tables are clearly illustrated on the Netscape Web site, at *http://home.netscape.com/assist/net_sites/tables.html*. With their more advanced features, HTML tables can provide not simply a way to present data clearly, but a strategy for Web page design itself. Examine the text *Connections* by Anderson, Benjamin, and Paredes-Holt for discussion of this strategy.

Frames

The frame feature gradually being supported by more and more Web browsers is a powerful tool for Web page organization and design. It supports the simultaneous presentation of multiple HTML pages, each in its own independently scrollable frame. With frames, a navigational tool such as an outline or timeline can remain constant in one frame, while various Web pages are loaded in the other frames. For information on the more complex features of HTML frames, examine an online tutorial, like those at *http://www.xmission.com/~fozz/ tutorials/frames.html* or *http://colos-www.prz.tu-berlin.de/~testcolo/ JAVASCRIPT/winframe.html.*

Frames are created by using the <FRAMESET> and </FRAMESET> tags, encompassing the <FRAME> tags which define the size and contents (file name or URL) of each of the frames. At the top level, an HTML document designed solely for the purpose defines how all the frames fit together. For example, consider the following script:

```
<FRAMESET ROWS="80%, 20%">
   <FRAMESET COLS="30%, 70%">
      <FRAME SRC=list.html NAME="listFrame">
      <FRAME SRC=content.html
        NAME="contentFrame">
   </FRAMESET>
   <FRAME SRC=navigate.html
      NAME="navigateFrame">
</FRAMESET>
```

Notice that three frames are defined, each one named (so further attributes can be given more easily to each of the frames) and given a source file ("SRC"). The various percentages describe proportions within the "rows" and "columns"—or the vertical and horizontal measures—of the browsing window. The script above produces a frame arrangement proportionate to the following:

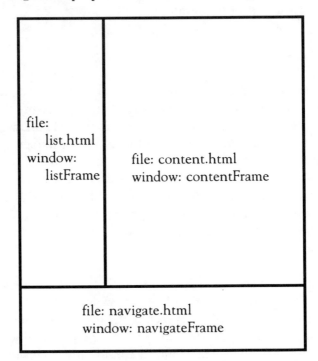

There is a hierarchy implied by the arrangement of the three frames within the script. The first tag assigns 80% of the "row" measure (the window's height) to the first frame following in the script—which is in this case a frameset consisting of two further frames (and closed with an ending tag). 20% of the height is assigned to the second frame ("navigateFrame"), which appears as a banner across the bottom of the window. Within the top frameset, meanwhile, 30% of the "column" or window width from the left margin is assigned to the first frame in the set, "listFrame." 70% of the width is assigned to the remaining frame, "contentFrame."

The linear logic to the script, therefore, proceeds from top to bottom, and left to right. Frames may be presented in a variety of arrangements; the key is paying attention to the ordering of <FRAMESET> and <FRAME> elements, and to the correct placement of ending tags.

Working With Sub-directories when Building Locally

The graphic below illustrates the paths necessary to work with sub-directories when building Web pages. As we explained in "Building Locally" (Chapter Six), it is only necessary to specify file and directory names when working on a local disk or drive to build Web pages.

However, if students wish to link to materials within a sub-directory or folder, they can specify the sub-directory, followed by a slash "/" and the file name.

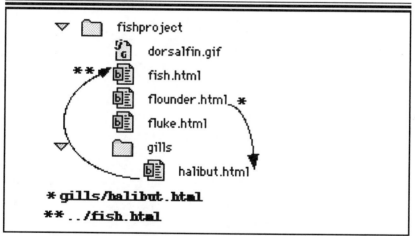

Local links using sub-directories

In the example above, the path "gills/halibut.html" links to a file called "halibut" which resides within a folder called "gills." To move back up in the directory structure, a link can use the "../" command

215

in a URL along with the path to the document or file to which you wish to connect. For example, to make a link from the file called "halibut.html" in the sample to the file "fish.html" in the directory directly above it in the hierarchy, a user would enter the URL "../fish.html." You can use a series of "/" and "../" commands to navigate through multiple directory levels. As with all links, students should name their files without spaces, and using lowercase characters.

Appendix Eight: Glossary

Anchor: 1.) the beginning point for a hypertextual link. Anchors usually use highlighted sections of text (hot text) or images to indicate links. 2.) in Web terminology, sometimes refers to the target destination for a link.

Application: any type of commercial, shareware or freeware computer program (usually with a user interface).

Archie: a protocol which allows keyword searches of the contents of FTP sites (primarily for names of freeware and shareware applications and graphic files).

ASCII Text: also known as "text only" format; ASCII characters are the basic numbers, letters and symbols supported by most types of computer operating systems.

AU: a sound file format commonly found on the World Wide Web.

Bookmark: an electronic pointer to a Gopher, FTP or Web site that can be recalled for future reference. A list of bookmarks is known as a "hotlist."

Boolean: 1.) logical search operators that allow a user to refine the scope of keyword searches. The simple Boolean operators are *and*, *or*, and *not*. 2.) flavoring used to make soup stock. Often small children will lick a Boolean cube for the salty flavor.

Bots (robots): objects in MU* environments which are programmed to interact with readers.

Channel: also referred to as a "line." An IRC channel is roughly equivalent to a C.B. radio frequency. Users join a channel to participate in the discussion that takes place among people logged on to that frequency.

Chat: 1.) a somewhat derogatory term used to describe newsgroups or listservs that are geared towards the discussion of nonacademic topics. 2.) a term often heard when talking about Internet Relay

Chat (IRC). The IRC channels are often called "chat lines" and the conversation that takes place on these channels is often referred to as "chat."

Clarinet: newsfeeds from Rueters and the Associated Press in the form of Usenet newsgroups. Institutions must pay a fee in order to subscribe to groups provided by the Clarinet company.

Client Software: software which communicates with a server to provide an easier interface for a user. (See Appendix Five for more client/server information).

Common Gateway Interface (CGI): a program which resides on a server and handles complex information requests. CGIs act as mediators between a source of information on a server, and a client. They are most commonly used to process forms in HTML.

Directory: a particular section of the basic organizational structure of a file system (known as a "folder" in some operating systems). Directories can contain any type of files, applications or other directories.

Domain: an element of an Internet or e-mail address designating an Internet organization, sub-organizations and the type of organization (e.g., **widgetinc.com**, or **utexas.edu**).

DOS®: see **Operating System.**

Downloading: retrieving a file or application from a remote host over the Internet.

E-mail (Electronic Mail): the basic form of Internet communication. E-mail is used to send all types of electronic correspondence to Internet-connected users around the world.

Emote: to virtually represent an action during the real-time conversations on IRCs and MU*s. For example, a user named Socrates could type `":listens intently."` and the text transmitted to other participants would read `"Socrates listens intently."`

Emoticons: "pictures" made of text symbols that express different emotions in e-mail messages, newsgroup postings, and real time discussions. The basic Internet emoticon is the "smiley," a sideways happy face. :-)

FAQ (Frequently Asked Questions): a file which collects and responds to some of the most common questions about a particular aspect of the Internet or about a particular topic (e.g., the FAQ file for BMW motorcycles).

File: any type of electronic document. Files can be in ASCII text, in a format for a particular program, or in a standardized format for sound, graphics or video (e.g., WAV, GIF, or MPEG).

Flame: usually a pejorative term describing a post that attacks a message or an individual. A flame usually has a confrontational tone and offers little or no constructive criticism.

Form: see **HTML Form**.

Freeware: software which can be downloaded without cost from the Internet.

FTP (File Transfer Protocol): an early system of downloading and uploading files across the Internet. Although somewhat basic FTP, is still frequently used.

GIF: Graphical Interchange Format, a graphics file format that is frequently used for images on the World Wide Web.

Gopher: a system of Internet protocols and directory structures that allows users to connect to remote hosts, to access directories of information, and to download files. In addition, Gopher sites can be searched for directory names, file titles, or text contained in individual files.

Gopher Client: a program which provides an easy interface for searching and accessing documents and directories in Gopherspace.

Gopherhost: see **Gopher Server**.

Gopher Server: also referred to as a "Gopherhost." A centralized server that offers hierarchically organized information to a user via a Gopher client.

Hardware: the mechanical parts of a computer system.

Hit: an item returned from a keyword search.

Home Page: conventional name given to a site on the World Wide Web. This name can be used for the central page both of a university or business site and for the personal page of an individual.

Host: 1.) an Internet-connected machine which serves files to various clients. 2.) any Internet-connected machine.

Hot Text: a hypertextual term which refers to a link anchored by a section of text. This is the most common way of linking documents on the Web. Hot text will generally appear in a different color or different style to indicate that clicking on it will take the user to another document.

Hotlist: see **Bookmark.**

HTML (Hypertext Markup Language): the scripting language which is used to turn plain text and other elements (such as images) into the integrated pages we see on the Web.

HTML Elements: HTML instructions, along with the text to which they apply: for example, the boldface text element, <B> . . . </B>, and the table element, <TABLE> . . . </TABLE>. Some HTML elements are "empty," meaning they do not have an ending tag or perform a function on particular text; for example, the <HR> element draws a horizontal rule across the page.

HTML Form: mechanism by which Web browsers allow users to send information back to a server. Forms can be used in a writing class to facilitate interaction between readers and authors of Web documents.

Freeware: software distributed free of charge.

HTML Headings: HTML commands which change the size of the text displayed in Web pages. Headings vary in size from <H1> through <H6> (largest to smallest) .

HTML Tags: HTML commands contained in angled brackets. Tags usually work in pairs, with a closing tag dictating where the selected text ends, but "empty" HTML elements, such as <HR>, do not have a closing tag.

HTTP (Hypertext Transport Protocol): an Internet protocol which allows for the transfer of files from a Web server to a Web client application.

Hypertexts: interactive documents that allow users to follow links to other documents and to present images, sound, and video.

Imagemap: an image which has been "mapped" by HTML commands so that clicking on different portions of it will link the user to different sites or files.

Index Page: the initial page of a site (or of a series of documents) which provides the organizational structure that maps the site—often the "starting point" for a hypertext.

Inline Image: an image which has been inserted into the design of a Web page.

Interface: the features of an application which mediate a user's interaction with the program. Generally speaking, the more intuitive the interface is to a user, the easier it will be to run the program.

IP Address (Internet Protocol Address): the address which is specific to a single computer and identifies it for the purpose of interacting with other computers on the Internet.

IRC (Internet Relay Chat): a system of Internet protocols and programs which allow users to participate on topic-centered, real-time discussion channels.

IRC Client: a program which provides an easy interface for a user who is logged on to an IRC channel.

Java: a programming language which grew out of experiments in software to connect different types of servers. Java is the basis of many interactive functions on Web pages, such as moving animations and the managing of complex information. These functions are actually performed by applications, or "applets," which reside on servers rather than individual PCs.

JPG/JPEG (from Joint Photographic Experts Group): a graphics file format that is frequently used for images on the World Wide Web.

Link: a hypertextual function that connects documents, sites, and other media. Note that "link" is commonly used both as a noun to indicate the actual connection between one node and another, and as a verb to indicate the process by which this connection is achieved.

Listproc: a type of mailing list software. See also **Listserv**.

Listserv: also known as a "mailing list" or "list." A program which allows mail to be sent to a group of addresses at once.

Local Area Network (LAN): a set of connections which allows a number of computers in a particular location to share files with each other. Most computer classrooms will be connected with a local area network.

Lurk: to read a newsgroup or e-mail list for a period of time without posting messages. This process is known as "lurking" because your presence is not known to the group unless you "speak up."

Macintosh® : see **Operating System.** See also **Platform.**

Mail Reader: also known as a "mail client." A program which provides an easy interface for reading, composing, posting and downloading e-mail messages.

Mail Server: an Internet server which organizes, stores and distributes e-mail messages.

Mailbox: the specific identification or name given to an e-mail user. Used in conjunction with the domain name, it makes up the e-mail address.

Majordomo: a type of mailing list software. See also **Listserv.**

Menu Command: a command that is executed by using a mouse to click on an option within a menu bar, a feature of both Macintosh® and Windows™ operating systems.

Modem: short for "modulater-demodulater," a device used to connect computers via a telephone line or other communication link to a network server. When you connect to the Internet at school your workstation may be directly wired to a server, but if you connect at home you will most likely need to use a modem.

Moderator: person responsible for determining the relevancy of messages posted to a moderated newsgroup or e-mail discussion list. A moderator will forward "appropriate" messages to the group.

Multipurpose Internet Mail Extensions (MIME): an encoding format which allows for the transfer of mixed-media data by electronic mail.

MUDs (also MUSHes, Tiny MUSHes, MOOs, etc.): text-based virtual spaces ("Multi User Dungeons" or "Domains") which allow users to interact in real-time with other users or with the textual environment. The different acronyms refer to different protocols which perform similar functions.

MUD Client: a program which provides an easy interface for a user who is logged onto a MUD.

MOV/MOOV: a video format often used on the World Wide Web.

MPG/MPEG: a video format often used on the World Wide Web.

News Host: see **News Server.**

News Server: also known as "News Host." An Internet-connected server which organizes, stores and distributes newsgroup messages.

Newsfeed: messages posted to a newsgroup which originate from a wire service or other traditional news source.

Newsgroups: topic-centered sites devoted to discussion and to the exchange of articles, messages, or other media. See also **Usenet.**

Newsreader: also known as a "news client." A program which provides an easy interface for reading, composing, posting and downloading newsgroup messages.

Nickname: 1.) similar to an address book entry for one or more e-mail addresses. When a message is sent to the nickname the computer sends that message to each of the addresses in the nickname file. 2.) a character name used to log on to IRC channels.

Node: a hypertextual site which organizes multiple links. Nodes can contain any combination of text, links, graphics, sound, and video.

Operating System: the software which controls the basic operations of the computer. Examples include Macintosh®, DOS®, and Unix. These systems are generally incompatible with each other.

PC: 1.) also referred to as "IBM compatibles," indicates computers which run DOS® operating systems (usually with the graphical user interface Windows™). 2.) less often used to indicate any personal computer.

Platforms: refers to computers with different types of operating systems, for example, Macintosh®, PC, or Unix.

Post: to send an electronic message to an e-mail discussion list or newsgroup. Also used as a noun to refer to the message itself.

Protocols: the "language" that a client and server use to distinguish various types of Internet media. E-mail, for example, relies on

Simple Mail Transfer Protocol (SMTP), while the Web uses Hypertext Transfer Protocol (HTTP).

Read-Only Memory (ROM): Information stored in chips or other media (e.g. CD-ROMs) that can only be read by a computer, not altered or written over.

Readme File: gives information about a piece of software or an Internet forum.

Real-time: refers to the almost instantaneous transfer of messages in IRCs and MU*s, allowing users to communicate in a way which resembles synchronous face-to-face conversation. Real-time can be seen in opposition to e-mail and newsgroup messages, which are asynchronous.

Reply Quotations: instead of using quotation marks or a block quote, most mail readers and newsreaders place a special character, usually an angled bracket (>), in front of a quotation in order to distinguish it from a new message. Most mail readers and newsreaders offer a "reply" function which will quote the whole text of the original message using this special character.

Robots: see **Bots.**

Root Directory: the uppermost directory in a directory hierarchy, designated by the slash symbol (/) in Unix and HTTP.

Scroll: to move up or down in a document using either the arrow keys or a mouse-driven scroll bar.

Search Engine: a device that performs keyword searches on the Internet (e.g., Veronica, WAIS, WebCrawler).

Server: 1.) simply put, software that provides information to client programs. Clients and servers "talk" to each other to allow the transfer of files and protocols across the Internet. 2.) commonly refers to the machine on which a server program is located.

Shareware: like "freeware," software which is made available through the Internet. The authors of shareware ask for a small licensing fee from users.

Signature File: pre-formatted text attached to the bottom of most e-mail and newsgroup messages which generally contains the author's name, e-mail address, and institutional affiliation (if any). Signature files often contain carefully constructed ASCII text pictures and favorite quotations.

Site License: an agreement which allows an organization to own and operate multiple copies of the same program.

Site: a collection of documents on the Internet providing information to users who access the location. Gopher sites and Web sites are the "places" designed by particular people or institutions to disseminate information. "Site" can refer to both a Web home page, for example, and the host machine on which it is located.

Slide Show: a series of textual screens that scroll by to deliver information in a MU*.

Software: computer programs written to perform various tasks, as opposed to "hardware" which refers to the mechanical parts of a computer system. See also **Application**.

Source Document: the underlying HTML document that produces a Web page when viewed with a Web browser. Most Web browsers allow a user to view the source document of any page found on the Web.

Subject Directory: hypertext index of Internet resources categorized by subject; featured on Gopher and Web research tools.

Surfing: the process of navigating from site to site on the Internet (usually the Web) in a nonlinear and non-hierarchical manner.

Targeting: connecting directly to a Gopherhost or Web site by entering a known address.

Telnet: a terminal emulation protocol. With a Telnet client application, you can establish a connection to a remote computer. Telnet refers both to the process of making "terminal emulation" connections on the Internet, and to the client applications which perform this function, such as NCSA Telnet.

Text Only: see **ASCII Text**.

Thread: a posting and a series of replies on the same topic, usually with the same subject heading.

Tunneling: accessing a site (usually a Gopher site) by digging down through various directories or sub-directories.

Unix: see **Operating System**. See also **Platform.**

Uploading: placing a file or application on a remote host over the Internet. Text, sound, graphics, video, and HTML files are uploaded to a Web server for publication.

URL (Uniform Resource Locator): the address assigned to each file on the World Wide Web.

Usenet: one subset of the Internet which facilitates the exchange of messages and discussion. Most colleges and universities are in-volved with Usenet newsgroups rather than private or commer-cial bulletin boards. The broad classification of Usenet contains thousands of topic-centered newsgroups organized hierarchically by name.

Veronica: a search engine which can locate items on most of the Internet's Gopher servers using keywords and Boolean operators.

WAIS (Wide Area Information Search): a search engine configured to locate and retrieve information from a designated set of docu-ments. Unlike Veronica or the Web search engines, WAIS per-forms local rather than general Internet searches.

WAV: a sound file format.

Web Browser: client software used for navigating and interacting with the World Wide Web. The Web browser translates the HTML source documents that reside on the Web into a fluid, multimedia interface.

Web Server: a server equipped with software to facilitate the Hypertext Transfer Protocol (HTTP) that enables documents to be linked and shared on the Web. Users can access the documents stored on Web servers with a Web browser.

Windows™: see **Operating System**.

Workstation: an individual computer usually connected to a net-work but primarily occupied by a single user. Used throughout this book to designate a personal computer where a user can operate local client software.

World Wide Web: abbreviated *WWW* or *the Web*. Distributed hypermedia system built upon older protocols (FTP, Gopher, etc.) and additional newer protocols (HTTP). WWW client soft-ware (see **Web Browser**) provides the ability to view many types of files (HTML, GIF, text, etc.).

Index

A

B

C

D

O

P

R

S

T

Targeting 102, 107–108
Telnet 22, 83, 84, 103, 104, 193-194, 199
Text Only. *See* ASCII Text
Thread 28, 42, 43, 49, 50, 54, 59
Tiny MUSH 91. *See also* MU*
Transcripts
  review of 76, 84, 142, 167
Tunneling 102, 106, 107, 108–109, 123, 125, 128-129

U

Unmoderated Discussion
  newsgroups 43-44, 47, 63
Uploading 138, 144, 151–152, 194, 195
URL 138, 140, 148, 149, 151, 156, 159
Usenet Newsgroup 3, 7, 41–59, 72, 73, 102, 103, 104, 108, 159

V

Veronica 110, 111-112, 126, 131, 133
Video 99, 106, 122, 144, 168-171
View Source. *See* Source Document

W

WAIS 110-111, 133
WebCrawler 100, 120-121, 132
Webcrawler 120
Workstation Client 197–200. *See* Client Software
World Wide Web
  browsers 56, 101, 104, 138, 140,
    143, 144, 145, 148, 149, 150, 151, 154, 157, 159, 200
  browsing 99–124
  composition 4, 137–161
  servers 143, 144, 148, 151-152, 154, 159
Writing Portfolio 54, 55
WWW Virtual Library 120

Y

Yahoo! 108, 116, 121, 149, 159